Conversion Tables

All quantities in the ingredients lists and recipes refer to the metric system. The recipes that were submitted in the imperial system were converted into the metric system and either rounded up or off.

Imperial	Metric	Imperial	Metric		Fahrenheit	Celsius
2 lb 4 oz	1 kg	1½ pints	1 L		475 °F	240 °C
1 lb 2 oz	500 g	18 fl oz	500 mL		425 °F	220 °C
14 oz	400 g	14 fl oz	400 mL		400 °F	200 °C
10½ oz	300 g	10 fl oz	300 mL		350 °F	180 °C
7 oz	200 g	7 fl oz	200 mL		325 °F	160 °C
3½ oz	100 g	3½ fl oz	100 mL		275 °F	140 °C
2½ oz	70 g	2 fl oz	50 mL			
2 oz	50 g		45 mL	3 tbsp		
1½ oz	40 g		30 mL	2 tbsp		
1½ oz	35 g		20 mL	1 tbsp		
1 oz	25 g		10 mL	3 tsp (1 tbsp)		
½ oz	10 g					

American Standard Measurements

The standard American measuring cup holds 8 fluid ounces, so approximately 225 mL, but one cup is also often used for roughly weighing 8 ounces (approximately 225 g) of rice, sugar, butter, or beans. Flour of all grades, mushrooms, and ground almonds weigh approximately 4 ounces (115 g) per cup.

Please note the difference between American standard liquid measurements (an American pint equals 16 fluid ounces) and imperial liquid measurements (an imperial pint equals 20 fluid ounces).

D1064237

Hubertus P. Bell, Tim Feuerstein, Carlos E. Güntner,
Sören Hölsken, J. Klaas Lohmann

What's Cooking in Chemistry?

How Leading Chemists Succeed in the Kitchen

Hubertus P. Bell, Tim Feuerstein, Carlos E. Güntner,
Sören Hölsken, J. Klaas Lohmann

What's Cooking in Chemistry?

How Leading Chemists Succeed in the Kitchen

WILEY-
VCH

WILEY-VCH GmbH & Co. KGaA

Authors

Hubertus P. Bell
Tim Feuerstein
Carlos E. Güntner
Sören Hölsken
J. Klaas Lohmann
Georg-August-Universität Göttingen
Institut für Organische Chemie
Tammannstraße 2
D-37077 Göttingen
Germany

Library of Congress Card No. applied for.

A catalog record for this book is available from the British Library.

Bibliographic information published by Die Deutsche Bibliothek
Die Deutsche Bibliothek lists this publication in the Deutsche Nationalbibliografie; detailed bibliographic data is available in the Internet at <http://dnb.ddb.de>.

1. Auflage 2003
  Nachdruck der 1. Auflage 2005

Printed in the Federal Republic of Germany.

Printed on acid-free paper.

Printing and Bookbinding:
Druckhaus »Thomas Müntzer«, Bad Langensalza

ISBN 3-527-30723-0

Dedicated to our mentor
Lutz Friedjan Tietze
on the occasion of his 60th birthday

Editorial

The passion for chemistry often goes together with a passion for good cuisine. Having this experience in mind, which resulted from the old tradition in our research group that everyone has to prepare an assortment of cakes for the others on the occasion of his birthday, we had the idea for this cookbook.

After inviting a number of well-known chemists from all around the world to participate in our project, we received the answers of some 60 professors who were inspired to send us a recipe, often together with some personal remarks about why they chose this particular one.

We are very grateful for their contributions that cover such different dishes as soups, meat, fish, sweet dishes, and even a punch. They are presented in this book together with short biographical and scientific sketches that might be interesting to read during the possible waiting times in the kitchen. Furthermore, we are indebted to M. Wöhrmann, who supported us in the beginning of this project, and to S. Stewart, who helped us while struggling for the right words. To A. Kühn and S. Schliebitz we owe the careful proofreading of the manuscript and to S. Hellkamp the software support. Finally, we thank G. Walter (Wiley-VCH) for the fruitful cooperation.

We wish you a lot of pleasure with this book, citing Georg C. Lichtenberg (1742–1799), professor of physics at Göttingen University: "Wer nichts als Chemie versteht, versteht auch die nicht recht." ("He who knows nothing but chemistry does not know chemistry either").

Göttingen 2003

Hubertus P. Bell
Tim Feuerstein
Carlos E. Güntner
Sören Hölsken
J. Klaas Lohmann

Contents

Martin Banwell

was born on November 24, 1954, in Lower Hutt, New Zealand. He
studied chemistry at the Victoria University of Wellington, where he
received his B.Sc. Hons. (1st class) in 1977 and his Ph.D. in Organic
Chemistry under the guidance of B. Halton in 1979. After a postdoc-
toral year with L. A. Paquette at the Ohio State University, Columbus,
he returned to the University of Adelaide, South Australia, as a Senior
Teaching Fellow at the Department of Organic Chemistry.
From 1993 to 1994 he was Associate Professor and Reader at the
University of Melbourne. Since 1999 he has been Professor at the
Australian National University in Canberra.
Among his fellowships and awards are the Rennie Medal of the Royal
Australian Chemical Institute (1986), the Grimwade Prize in Industrial
Chemistry (1992), and the Humboldt Research Award of the
Alexander von Humboldt Foundation (2000). He was elected Fellow
of the Royal Australian Chemical Institute in 1992, a Fellow of the
Japan Society for the Promotion of Science in 1999, and an Honorary
Fellow of the Royal Society of New Zealand in 2000. Moreover, he is
a member of the Honorary Advisory Board of *Synlett* (since 1997), the
International Advisory Editorial Board of the *New Journal of Chemistry*
(since 1997), the Editorial Board of the *Indian Journal of Chemistry,
Section B* (since 1999), and an Associate Editor of the *Journal of the
Chemical Society, Perkin Transaction 1* (since 1999) and of *Methods in
Organic Synthesis* (since 1999).
He is author of approximately 150 papers in refereed journals; five
patents have been issued to him.

Scientific Sketch

The research activities of Banwell's group are focused on developing new and efficient methodologies for the synthesis of target molecules ranging from biologically active natural products to compounds having unusual architectures that could be exploited for molecular recognition or materials science purposes. Natural products that have been targeted for synthesis include various anti-mitotic agents such as paclitaxel (Taxol™) (*J. Chem. Soc., Chem. Commun.* **1995**, 1395) and lamellarin K (Fig. 1), an alkaloid isolated from a Pacific ascidian collected at the northeastern coast of Australia (*J. Chem. Soc., Chem. Commun.* **1997**, 2259).

Figure 1. Lamellarin K (**1**).

The former compound is used clinically for the treatment of ovarian and breast cancers, while the latter shows great potential for combating multidrug-resistant cancers. The group's recently completed and highly convergent synthesis of compound **1** is now being adapted to the solid-phase to allow the generation of analogue libraries. Such libraries will be used to probe the structure/activity profile of this class of natural products and to construct novel hybrids with the colchicinoid class of anti-mitotic agents. In collaboration with Australian companies, Banwell is also engaged in developing concise syntheses of the polyketide herbicide herboxidiene (*Pure Appl. Chem.* **2000**, 72, 1631) and various analogues of the anti-influenza drug GG-167.

A second research focus involves compounds of the general structure shown in Fig. 2 which are obtained in multi-gram quantities and enantiomeric excesses of more than 99.8% by microbial oxidation of the corresponding aromatic.

Figure 2. *cis*-Dihydrocatechols **2** obtained by microbial oxidation.

These *cis*-1,2-dihyrocatechols embody unusual combinations of functionalities, and they are used as starting materials for the synthesis of a wide range of compounds including (+)- and (−)-steroids, (+)- and (−)-taxoids, pyrethroids, carbohydrates (e.g., vitamin C), and triquinoid natural products (*J. Chem. Soc., Perkin Trans. 1* **2002**, 2439). Another broad area of activity is concerned with exploiting ring-fused *gem*-dihalogenocyclopropanes in chemical syntheses. These compounds, which are readily obtained via dihalocarbene addition to the corresponding cycloalkene, serve as a useful starting material for the synthesis of various natural products (*J. Org. Chem.* **2000**, 65, 4241). In addition, Banwell and coworkers have recently discovered that such compounds undergo a novel dimerization reaction, which allows the construction of molecular clefts possessing convergent functional groups. Certain of these clefts have shown an ability to "recognize" carbohydrates and are now "tuned" to optimize this recognition process. The longer term objective is to develop systems that might be used for diagnostic/analytical purposes. Furthermore, these clefts may serve as catalysts for various cycloaddition reactions.

Marinade for BBQ Kangaroo

Starting materials (serves 4):

2 tbsp soy sauce

1 tbsp "Blue Gum" honey (almost any honey will suffice)

1 tbsp light virgin olive oil

1 tbsp tomato sauce

1 piece (ca. 10 g) peeled root ginger

2 cloves garlic

500 g kangaroo loin (or fillet of beef)

Add the soy sauce, honey, oil, tomato sauce, and diced ginger to a generous-sized plastic container, then squeeze in the juice from the garlic cloves. "Striploin" fillet of kangaroo cut into small to medium portions is then added to the marinade and the mixture is stirred thoroughly so as to ensure that the entire surface of the meat is covered. Seal the container and store in the refrigerator for approximately 7–10 hours with occasional shaking.

The meat is removed from the marinade and immediately cooked on a BBQ (or in a fry pan) with a hot flame until (in the case of kangaroo, at least) rare to medium rare. The residual marinade can be used to baste the meat while it is cooking.

Serve the meat with a fresh green salad, corn on the cob, and a red wine (a McLaren Vale Shiraz from South Australia is especially appropriate).

«Kangaroo is a very lean, popular, and readily available meat in Australia. The marinade can also be used with beef. Using eucalyptus (gum tree) leaves and twigs as part of the BBQ fuel imparts an additional quality to the meat that many people enjoy.»

Martin Banwell

Robert G. Bergman

was born in Chicago on May 23, 1942. After completing his undergraduate studies in chemistry at Carleton College in 1963, he received his Ph.D. at the University of Wisconsin in 1966 under the direction of J. A. Berson. While at Wisconsin he was awarded a National Institutes of Health (NIH) Predoctoral Fellowship. Bergman spent 1966 and 1967 as a NATO Fellow in R. Breslow's laboratories at Columbia, and following that went to the California Institute of Technology as a Noyes Research Instructor. He was promoted to assistant professor in 1969, associate professor in 1971, and full professor in 1973. He accepted an appointment as Professor of Chemistry at the University of California, Berkeley, in 1977, where he was appointed Gerald E. K. Branch Distinguished Professor in 2002. During his long scientific career, Bergman has received many awards and honors, which include the ACS Award in Organometallic Chemistry (1986), the Arthur C. Cope Scholar Award (1987), the E. F. Smith Award (1990), the I. Remsen Award (1990), a MERIT Award from the NIH (1991), the E. O. Lawrence Award in Chemistry from the U.S. Department of Energy (1994), the ACS Arthur C. Cope Award (1996), a Guggenheim Fellowship (1999), the American Institute of Chemists Chemical Pioneer Award (1999), the E. Leete Award for Teaching and Research in Organic Chemistry (2001), and a number of visiting professorships. He will soon receive the 2003 ACS James Flack Norris Award in Physical Organic Chemistry. Bergman is a member of the National Academy of Sciences (since 1984) and the American Academy of Arts and Sciences (since 1984) and has served on many academic and administrative committees and review boards. He has been or is currently a member of the Editorial Advisory Boards of several scientific journals (e.g., *Journal of Organic Chemistry, Organometallics, Chemical Reviews, International Journal of Chemical Kinetics, Synlett,* and *Organic Letters*).

Scientific Sketch

Research in the Bergman group centers on organic and organometallic reactions that take place in homogeneous solution. Bergman's early work in physical organic chemistry led to the discovery of the so-called "Bergman cyclization." In this process, *cis*-enediynes cyclize when heated to generate 1,4-benzenoid diradicals (Fig. 1), which then abstract hydrogen or halogen atoms to give stable aromatic products (*Acc. Chem. Res.* **1973**, *6*, 25).

Figure 1. Thermal cyclization/aromatization of cis-hex-3-ene-1,5-diyne.

In his more recent studies, Bergman has focused on organometallic chemistry and homogeneous catalysis. Bergman's primary goals are to develop new stoichiometric and catalytic processes and to gain fundamental understanding of their mechanisms. One major effort is directed toward carbon-hydrogen (C-H) bond activation reactions. This involves the development and study of metal complexes that undergo intermolecular oxidative addition with the normally inert C-H bonds in alkanes and other organic molecules.

Cyclized products:

dr = 15:1

Figure 2. Ring-closure reactions catalyzed by Rh(1) that employ a C-H-activation step.

This process holds potential for converting methane and other hydrocarbons into useful functionalized organic molecules. Recent efforts have yielded directed catalytic C-H activation reactions that lead to efficient cyclization of a variety of organic substrates (Fig. 2, *J. Am. Chem. Soc.* **2001**, *123*, 2685).

A second major area of investigation involves the study of the mechanisms of metal-mediated atom- and group-transfer processes using organometallic complexes having metal-oxygen, -nitrogen, and -sulfur bonds. Recent efforts in this area have yielded early transition metal imido (M=NR) complexes that undergo highly enantioselective cycloaddition reactions between metal-nitrogen multiple bonds and substituted allenes, (Fig. 3, *Angew. Chem. Int. Ed.* **2000**, *39*, 2339) and the discovery of complexes with exceptionally basic nitrogen ligands.

Residual allene enantioselectivity:

R	R'	% ee
Ph	Ph	>98
n-Pr	n-Pr	>98
Ph	Me	94
Ph	Et	>98
i-Pr	Me$_3$Si	>95

Figure 3. The use of enantioresolved imido complexes in the kinetic resolution of chiral allenes.

These reactions are being applied to the development of efficient catalytic carbon-nitrogen bond-forming processes such as carbon-carbon multiple bond hydroamination reactions. Other projects in the group are directed at the design and synthesis of novel ligands for transition metal centers, and heterobinuclear complexes, that should provide entries to new and more selective catalytic transformations. Density functional theory is being used to supplement understanding obtained from mechanistic experiments and to help determine the direction of new experimental work.

Potato Latkes (Potato Pancakes): A Traditional Jewish Chanukah Dish

Starting materials:

6 large potatoes

1 small onion

2 eggs

3 tbsp flour

¼ tsp pepper

1 tsp salt

1 tsp baking soda

Peel the potatoes and store them in a bowl of cold water to keep them from oxidizing. Grate the potatoes and onion as quickly as possible. Separate the liquid. Add the other ingredients and mix well. The consistency should be somewhat thick; add more flour if it seems too runny. Pour 60 mL oil into heated frying pan. When the oil bubbles, spoon pancake-sized portions onto a hot, pre-greased skillet. Turn when golden brown. Be sure to add fresh oil as needed so the potatoes do not burn. When both sides are golden brown, remove the latkes with a slotted spatula so that the oil will drain off, and layer on a plate between paper towels, which will absorb more oil. Continue until all of the potato batter is used. Serve hot with applesauce or sour cream.

«In the second century B.C., the inhabitants of Judea joined a rebellion against the kingdom of Antiochus IV under the leadership of a country priest named Mattathais and his five sons (of whom Judah became the most famous, known as "the hammer" or Maccabee). The Maccabees and their followers used guerrilla tactics to win the first national liberation struggle in recorded history. In 165 B.C. they retook Jerusalem, purified and rededicated the Temple, which had been vandalized and desecrated, and rekindled the eternal light, which is always to be kept burning. They had only a small amount of oil, but the holiday of Chanukah (which means "dedication") was established to commemorate the legend that this small amount of oil kept the eternal light burning for eight days.

Potato latkes (potato pancakes) are a dish that Jews traditionally serve during the Chanukah holiday. It is certainly not clear that potatoes were available in ancient times, so the dish was probably developed in eastern Europe. The latkes are cooked in oil, another means of commemorating the eternal light legend.»

Robert G. Bergman

Dale L. Boger

was born on August 22, 1953 in Hutchinson, Kansas. He received his B.Sc. in chemistry from the University of Kansas, Lawrence, Kansas (1975, with highest distinction and honors in chemistry), and his Ph.D. in chemistry from Harvard University (1980) under the direction of E. J. Corey. He returned to the University of Kansas as a member of the faculty in the Department of Medicinal Chemistry (1979–1985), moved to the Department of Chemistry at Purdue University (1985–1991), and joined the faculty in the newly created Department of Chemistry at The Scripps Research Institute (1991–present) as the Richard and Alice Cramer Professor of Chemistry. Among Dale Boger´s numerous awards and honors are the ACS Arthur C. Cope Scholar Award (1988), the American Cyanamide Academic Award (1989), the ISCH Katritzky Award in Heterocyclic Chemistry (1997), the Aldrich ACS Award for Creativity in Organic Synthesis (1999), the A. R. Day Award (2000), and the Paul Janssen Award for Creativity in Organic Synthesis (2002). Since 1990 he has been editor of *Bioorganic and Medicinal Chemistry Letters* and a member of the advisory board of the *Journal of Organic Chemistry*.

Scientific Sketch

The research interests of Boger's group include the total synthesis of biologically active natural products, the development of new synthetic methods, heterocyclic chemistry, bioorganic and medicinal chemistry, combinatorial chemistry, the study of DNA-agent interactions, and the chemistry of antitumor antibiotics. Boger places a special emphasis on investigations to define the structure-function relationships of natural or designed agents in an effort to understand the origin of their biological properties.

As new synthetic methodologies, the Boger group has developed acyl radical reactions, which are useful tools in natural product total synthesis. Selenyl ketones are used as precursors of acyl radicals. The radical, which is formed after reaction with the double/triplebond, can be saturated with Bu₃SnH (Fig. 1, *J. Am. Chem. Soc.* **1990**, *112*, 4003).

Figure 1. Cyclization of acyl radicals.

The enantiomer of roseophilin, an antitumor antibiotic, was synthesized in Boger's group recently. It possesses a topologically unique pentacyclic skeleton, and its complex structure is a challenge for an organic chemist. The key steps are a heterocyclic azadiene *Diels-Alder* reaction, a ring-closing metathesis, and a stereoselective acyl radical cyclization. (Fig. 2, *J. Am. Chem. Soc.* **2001**, *123*, 8515).

Figure 2. Total synthesis of ent-(−)-roseophilin.

Another important research topic is the biology and chemistry of CC-1065 and the duocarmycins and their derivatives. These natural products bind in the minor groove of the double helix and alkylate DNA bases irreversibly according to the mechanism displayed in Fig. **3**.

Figure 3. Mechanism for the alkylation of DNA bases by duocarmycin SA.

Cannoli Shells

Starting materials (makes 25):

450 mL unsifted, regular all-purpose flour

½ tsp salt

2 tbsp granulated sugar

I egg, slightly beaten

2 tbsp firm butter, cut into small pieces

about 60 mL dry Sauterne

I egg white, slightly beaten

shortening or salad oil for deep-frying

ricotta filling (see below)

powered sugar

chopped sweet chocolate

Ricotta filling:

I kg (I L) ricotta cheese

375 mL powdered sugar

4 tsp vanilla

60 mL sweet chocolate

Fluffy ricotta filling:

500 g (500 mL) ricotta cheese

200 g powdered sugar

2 tsp vanilla

30 mL sweet chocolate

250 mL heavy cream

Sift flour with salt and granulated sugar. Make a well in the center; in it, place the egg and butter. Stir with a fork, working from the center out, to moisten the flour mixture. Add the wine, one tablespoon at a time, until the dough begins to cling together. Use your hands to form the dough into a ball. Cover it and let it stand for 15 minutes.

Roll dough out on a floured board about 2 mm thick, cut into three 1.3-cm circles. With a rolling pin, roll the circle into ovals. Wrap them around hollow metal cannoli forms and seal the edge with egg white. Turn out the ends of the dough and flare them slightly. Fry two or three at a time in deep hot fat (180 °C) for about 1 minute or until lightly golden. Remove them with tongs to a paper towel to drain; let them cool about 5 seconds, then slip them out of the cannoli form, holding the shell carefully. Cool the shells completely before filling them with a pastry tube. Sift powdered sugar over shell; garnish at ends. Makes 25.

Ricotta filling: Whirl 1 kg ricotta cheese in a blender, or press through wire strainer, until very smooth. Fold in 375 mL unsifted powdered sugar and 4 tsp vanilla. Mix in 60 mL sweet chocolate (optional). Chill several hours.

Fluffy ricotta filling: Prepare ½ recipe Ricotta Filling, then fold in 250 mL heavy cream that has been whipped until stiff.

«As a young group and as my career was beginning, we developed a tradition of preparing cannoli for dessert at group gatherings. This included an annual Thanksgiving Day gathering that continues to this day and a gathering to watch the Super Bowl game on Super Bowl Sunday. Group members would take their turn at rolling the dough, cutting the ovals, or deep-frying the shells. We came to learn that success in the lab did not always translate into thin, crispy cannoli shells, but the yield was always reproducible.»

Dale Boger

Carsten Bolm

was born on March 8, 1960 in Braunschweig, Germany. He studied chemistry at the Technical University Braunschweig and at the University of Wisconsin, Madison, where he performed research under the supervision of H. Hopf and H.-J. Reich, respectively. In 1984 he received a M. Sc. degree in Madison and obtained a diploma in Brunswick. He then moved to the University of Marburg to start his doctoral work under the guidance of M. T. Reetz. After a postdoctoral stay in 1987/8 with K. B. Sharpless at the M.I.T. in Cambridge, Massachusetts, he worked in Basel with B. Giese to obtain his habilitation in 1993. In the same year, he was appointed Professor of Organic Chemistry at the University of Marburg. Since 1996 he has held a Chair of Organic Chemistry at the RWTH Aachen. Carsten Bolm was Visiting Professor in Madison, Florence, Paris, and Milan. Among several awards, he received the Heinz Maier Leibnitz Award (1991), the ADUC-Prize (1992), the Otto Klung Award (1996), and the Otto Bayer Award (1998). He is a member of the advisory boards of *Advanced Synthesis & Catalysis*, *New Journal of Chemistry*, *Synthesis*, and *Synlett*. Furthermore, he published the book *Transition Metals for Organic Synthesis* (Wiley-VCH, 1998) together with M. Beller.

Scientific Sketch

The major focus of Bolm's research is on asymmetric metal catalysis, synthesis with organometallic reagents, and pseudopeptides.

Asymmetric synthesis has successfully been used for the preparation of enantiopure pharmaceuticals or agrochemicals. Within this area, catalytic approaches are considered most favorable. Catalysts of such type usually consist of a metal center and a ligand bearing the stereochemical information (Fig. 1), which ensures that the bond-forming process proceeds in a stereoselective manner.

1

Figure 1. Bolm´s ferrocene (S,R_p)-**1**.

In this context, one of the major research targets of Professor Bolm is to find and develop ligands and metal complexes with multiple stereogenic elements for the catalytic enantioselective addition of zinc reagents to aldehydes

and imine derivatives (Fig. **2**, *J. Org. Chem.* **1998**, *63*, 7860; *Angew. Chem. Int. Ed.* **2000**, *39*, 3465). In particular, aryl transfer reactions have been studied that lead to synthetically important diaryl methanols (**3**) and diaryl methyl amines with excellent enantiomeric excesses (*Angew. Chem. Int. Ed.* **2001**, *40*, 1488; *Angew. Chem. Int. Ed.* **2002**, *41*, 3692).

Figure 3. Basic pseudotripeptide structure.

Another field of his work is focused on peptide mimetics. Due to their poor bioavailability and rapid enzymatic degradation, peptides have found only limited application as pharmaceuticals. Thus, Professor Bolm uses sulfoximines as chiral backbone-modifying elements to prepare new pseudopeptides with higher stability against enzymatic degradation. By this strategy, new enzyme inhibitors could result (Fig. **3**; *Chem. Eur. J.* **2001**, *7*, 1118; *Org. Lett.* **2002**, *4*, 893).

Figure 2. Asymmetric phenyl transfer onto substituted benzaldehydes in the presence of catalytic amounts of Bolm´s ferrocene (S,R_p)-**1**.

Kaiserschmarren
From the King's Hight in the Emperor's City

Starting materials (serves 6):

Stewed fruits:

50 g raisins

10 mL (1 tbsp) rum

250 g sour cherries

170 g sugar

125 mL white wine

Dough:

6 eggs

60 g sugar

pinch of salt

1 g lemon zest

12 mL (1 tbsp) double cream

65 g flour

butter

Soak raisins (50 g) overnight at room temperature in rum (10 mL) in a 50-mL screw cap vessel, which should occasionally be shaken. Next, fill sour cherries (250 g) into a 250-mL beaker and add sugar (60 g) and white wine (125 mL). Cover the reaction mixture and store cool overnight.

To synthesize the dough, whisk 6 eggs (weight class 2), sugar (60 g), fine lemon zest, and double cream (12 mL) with a dough mixer (KPG-mixer) at ca. 600 rpm in a 2-L porcelain bowl. Then add flour (65 g) and leave the dough to rise for 30 minutes.

Heat butter (50 g) carefully in a frying pan and add some of the dough (CAUTION: squirting). Fry until golden underneath, then, using a fork, tear into small pieces (ca. 1 cm) and brown, turning frequently, and keep it warm in a muffle furnace.

Synthesis of stewed fruits: In a beaker, sugar is caramelized in molten butter (50 g). Using a Büchner funnel, filter off the sour cherries and raisins and then stir them into the caramel mixture. Quench the mixture with the filtrate (cherry juice/wine mixture). Pour the stewed fruits over the warm Kaiserschmarren, add some drops of orange liqueur, and dust the solid with icing sugar (3 g). Before serving, decorate with some lemon balm leafs.

Ronald Breslow

was born in Rahway, New Jersey, on March 14, 1931. His chemical career started with undergraduate and graduate training at Harvard University, where he also did his Ph.D. research with R. B. Woodward. He then spent a year in Cambridge, England, as a postdoctoral fellow with Lord A. R. Todd and came to Columbia University in 1956 as Instructor in Chemistry, where he now holds the chair of the Samuel Latham Mitchill Professor of Chemistry. He is also University Professor, one of 12 at Columbia, and member and honorary member of several learned societies, among those the U.S. National Academy of Sciences, the American Academy of Arts and Sciences, the American Philosophical Society, the New York Academy of Sciences, the Royal Society of Chemistry (UK), the Royal Society (UK), the World Innovation Foundation, and the Chemical Society of Japan. His research is published in more than 400 papers and was acknowledged with numerous scientific awards, among those the ACS Award in Pure Chemistry (1966), the Fresenius Award of Phi Lambda Upsilon (1966), the Remsen Prize (1977), the Roussel Prize in Steroids (1978), the ACS James Flack Norris Award in Physical Organic Chemistry (1980), the Arthur C. Cope Award (1987), the Kenner Award (1988), the Nichols Medal (1989), the National Academy of Sciences Award in Chemistry (1989), the Allan Day Award (1990), the Paracelsus Award and Medal of the Swiss Chemical Society (1990), and the U.S. National Medal of Science (1991). He was recently named one of the top 75 contributors to the chemical enterprise in the past 75 years by *Chemical & Engineering News* (1997) and won the Priestley Medal (1999). In 2000 he won the New York City Mayor's Award in Science, and in 2002 he received the ACS Bader Award in Bioorganic or Bioinorganic Chemistry and the Esselen Award for Chemistry in the Public Interest. He served as president of the American Chemical Society (in 1996) and belongs to the editorial board of a number of scientific journals.

Scientific Sketch

Breslow's research interests involve on the one hand the design and synthesis of new molecules with interesting properties, and on the other hand the study of these properties. Examples include the cyclopropenyl cation, the simplest aromatic system and the first aromatic compound prepared with other than six electrons in a ring. His work establishing the phenomenon of anti-aromaticity has involved the synthesis and characterization of novel molecules. Even in the work on purely mechanistic questions, such as the discovery of the chemical mechanism of thiamine (vitamin B-1) in biochemical reactions, the synthesis and study of novel molecules has played an important role. Although he continues his interest in unusual conjugated systems, his major emphasis in recent years has been associated with the understanding of mechanisms in enzymes and enzyme model systems and the development of good artificial enzymes. Some work is focused on understanding the detailed mechanisms of carboxypeptidases and ribonucleases and some on the enzymes that utilize coenzyme B12 as a cofactor. Based on this experience, new artificial enzymes are produced by combining good binding sites, such as hydrophobic pockets of cyclodextrins, with appropriately placed catalytic groups. Recently, Breslow has shown the power of artificial cytochrome P-450 enzymes for catalytic oxidations of steroid substrates (Fig. 1, *J. Org. Chem.* **2002**, *67*, 5057).

Figure 1. Catalytic oxidations of steroid substrates by artificial enzymes.

An example that also demonstrates the second major effort of Breslow and coworkers is the application of templates (see Fig. 1, group R^1) that achieve geometric control of the point of attack on a complex molecule, resulting in regio-specificity (see also *Chemtracts Org. Chem.* **2002**, *15*, 59). Investigations of the complex geometries are supported by molecular and computational models.

Figure 2. An effective cancer cell differentiating agent.

Beside the synthesis of artificial enzymes, Breslow and coworkers study the physical effects of reactions, e.g., the antihydrophobic cosolvent effects for alkylation reactions in water solutions (*J. Am. Chem. Soc.* **2002**, *124*, 3622), as well as the development of a computational model to probe the relative hydrophobicity of aromatic surfaces.

Breslow is also interested in developing new agents against cancer. He has shown an approach of using cyclodextrine dimers for a photodynamic therapy (*J. Am. Chem. Soc.* **2001**, *123*, 12488) and is involved in a fruitful collaboration with Marks and Rifkind at the Sloan Kettering Institute for Cancer Research. Here they have developed cytodifferentiating agents for cancer chemotherapy, that are able to induce undifferentiated or de-differentiated cells to transform to an adult noninvasive form (Fig. 2, *Helv. Chim. Acta* **2000**, *83*, 1685).

Veal and Sausage Stew

Starting materials:

425 g veal sausage (Italian style, with anise)

425 g veal chunks

425 g sliced mushrooms

425 g sliced carrots

2 large onions

2 cloves garlic

2 bay leaves

chopped parsley

salt

pepper

red or white wine

olive oil

pasta

salad

In a coverable kettle, sauté the veal sausage (cut into bite-sized chunks) in a little olive oil and pour off the fat when it is done. Remove it to a bowl, and sauté the onions, the chopped garlic, and the veal chunks in more olive oil until they are brown, then remove to the bowl. Add the sliced mushrooms and cook until the water is driven off, return the meat and onions to the pot, and cover the contents with ordinary red or white wine and simmer (covered) for at least two hours after adding two bay leaves, a handful of chopped parsley, some salt and pepper, and the sliced carrots. Then cool the stew and reheat it before serving (it is much better after this cooling and reheat cycle, which brings the sauce into the meat; for this reason, the stew is even better the second day). Serve with appropriate pasta and a good salad.

«A variation incorporates some tomatoes as well before the simmering step. In another variation, uncooked peas are added 10 minutes before the end of the simmering step. The garlic should have its bitter core removed before chopping.»

Ronald Breslow

Reinhard Brückner

was born on May 5, 1955 in Braunschweig, Germany. He studied chemistry at the University of Munich and obtained his Ph.D. in 1984 under the guidance of R. Huisgen. After a postdoctoral stay with P. A. Wender at Stanford University in 1985, he joined the chemistry faculty at the University of Marburg for his habilitation with R. W. Hoffmann. In 1991 he became an associate professor at the University of Würzburg before joining the chemistry faculty at the University of Göttingen as full professor in 1992. Since 1998 he has held a chair of organic chemistry at the University of Freiburg. Brückner was a visiting professor at the universities of Wisconsin/Madison in 1990 and Santiago de Compostela (Spain) in 1995. Among several awards, he received the Chemistry Award of the Academy of Science in Göttingen (1990) and the Literature Award of the Fonds der Chemischen Industrie (1998) for his textbook "*Reaktionsmechanismen – Organische Reaktionen, Stereochemie, moderne Synthesemethoden*" (Spektrum, 1996), which was translated into English ("*Advanced Organic Chemistry*", Harlekijn, 2001) and French ("*Mécanismes Réactionnels en Chimie Organique*", De Boeck, 1999) and which appeared as an enlarged second edition in 2002.

Scientific Sketch

Brückner´s research interests are the total synthesis of natural products, the synthesis of biologically active analogues thereof, and – in the context of this work – the development of efficient methodology.

The anti-cancer agent neocarzinostatin chromophore (1), which prevents the proliferation of cancer cells through the formation of DNA-cleaving biradicals, was modeled through the synthesis of an epoxide- and carbonate-containing dienediyne (2) (Fig. 1, *Liebigs Ann./Recueil* 1997, 961). This compound and related ones (*Synthesis* 2000, 588) were obtained from enol triflates for which stereoselective accesses were found.

Figure 1. Enediynes.

Skipped polyols have been another synthetic goal of the Brückner group. The permethylated 1,3,5,7,9-pentaol (3) was reached in a variety of ways (Fig. 2, *Liebigs Ann./Recueil* 1997, 1635, 1645, 1657, 1667) that are currently adapted to the total synthesis of some polyol,polyene antibiotics.

Figure 2. Pentaether from *Tolypothrix.*

In recent years, Brückner and coworkers prepared γ-chiral butanolides and γ-chiral butenolides starting with the asymmetric dihydroxylation of trans-configured β,γ-unsaturated carboxylic esters. The stereostructure of montecristin, which is such a compound and biogenetically is the precursor of several antitumor and antiparasitic agents, emerged from a synthesis of its unnatural enantiomer (4, Fig. 3, *New J. Chem.* 2001, 40).

Figure 3. Final steps in the synthesis of a γ-chiral butenolide.

Another part of Brückner´s group synthesizes γ-alkylidenebutenolides by an *anti*-elimination route (*J. Chem. Soc., Chem. Commun.* 2001, 141, *Curr. Org. Chem.* 2001, 4, 679). This domain includes the first synthesis of xerulin (5, Fig. 4, *Synlett* 1999, 1227), which inhibits the biosynthesis of cholesterol, a stereoselective synthesis of lissoclinolide (6, Fig. 4, *Synthesis* 1999, 1520), and the development of a strategy for the synthesis of peridinin, which is a carotinoid butenolide and a light-harvesting entity of sea plankton (*Synlett* 2000, 374).

Figure 4. γ-Alkylidenebutenolide target structures.

Pears, Beans and Bacon

Starting materials (serves 4):

250 g streaky, smoked bacon

¾ L broth

500 g beans (French beans)

1 bunch savory

500 g potatoes

500 g small pears

some flour or starch

pepper, salt, and a pinch sugar

Boil the chopped bacon in the broth for approximately 15 minutes. Clean the beans and break them into pieces of about 4 cm. Add the beans, the savory, and the bacon and let it boil for a further 15 minutes. Chop the potatoes and cut them into cubes. Clean the pears and remove the cores. Add the potatoes and quartered pears to the beans and simmer for 15 minutes.

Bind the stew with flour or starch until the desired consistency is obtained and season with pepper, salt, and a pinch of sugar.

«Are there any people of advanced age who do not like to eat? Probably not many, and I don't belong to those. Are there any people who do not like to cook? Probably a lot – among them even chemists – and I belong to this group. In nutrition-poor emergency situations, I rely on bread and butter, fried eggs, or pasta with ketchup forwards and backwards. While preparing those dishes, I hold not a cookbook in my hands but the sports section of my daily newspaper, or a thriller, or, of course, a chemistry book, because where kitchen fails, intellect needs all the more motivating food.

But neither butter and bread nor fried eggs constitute a suitable preparation procedure for this book. Fortunately, I can refer to an event which took place many years ago: During my studies in Munich, I met my future wife, and to impress her – to impress her even more – I thought of extraordinary activities! So, let´s say it was male courtship behavior that let me swing the wooden spoon to reach my personal cooking peak. As a matter of course, I asked my mother – an experienced cook from Northern Germany – and she sent me this traditional recipe from Lower Saxony through the phone.

Apparently there are versions in which the bacon is boiled in one piece and just cut into slices before serving. This seemed to be too risky to me, as I had to go back and forth between the small kitchen of my landlady and my furnished room at that time and the steaming mulligan stew was expected to appear on the table as if by magic. Some people argue that the pears and even the potatoes should be boiled separately. But be careful: this means there are *several* pots to be cleaned afterwards. I can imagine small pearl-pears to be more beautiful, but – as I can tell you confidentially – even pears out of a can could not prevent her from saying "Yes".»

Reinhard Brückner

Father, daugther, and baked-peas soup (the latter is available also as an instant meal).

Gianfranco Cainelli

was born in Trento, Italy, on June 8, 1932. In 1954 he became graduate engineer and in 1958, Ph.D. at the ETH Zürich working in the laboratory of O. Jeger. After two years as a postdoctoral fellow in the same group, he moved to the Politecnico of Milan as an assistant to A. Quilico and in 1968 joined the faculty of Pharmacy at the University of Bari, Italy, as full professor of natural product chemistry. Since 1971 he has been Professor of Organic Chemistry at the University of Bologna. He obtained the Gold Medal of the Italian President of the Republic for the "Benemeriti della scienza e della cultura" and the Quilico Gold Medal, and he has been Ziegler-Natta Lecturer (2002). His research is documented in some 152 publications and 20 patents.

Scientific Sketch

Cainelli's chemical interest concerns isolation and determination of the structure of natural products as well as developing synthetic methods for the synthesis of natural products. Pentacyclic triterpenes and trisporic acids (metabolites of *Choanephora trispora*) were isolated by his group recently.

Partial synthesis of aldosterone, androsterone, and nor-androsterone; total synthesis of beta-lactam antibiotics (carbapenems PS5 and PS6); chiral intermediates for penems and carbapenems (Fig. I, *Synthesis* **2000**, 289); total synthesis of vitamin A and abscissic acid; and synthesis of prostaglandins have been realized:

Figure I. Synthesis of the lactam I.

Synthesis and reactivity of geminal organometallic compounds have been investigated in Cainelli's group, aluminum-aluminum, boron-boron, lithium-boron, and magnesium-magnesium showing for the first time that they behave like *Wittig*-reagents. α-Lithium-halogen compounds have also been studied.

Several reagents supported on cross-linked polystyrene have been prepared for the first time, e.g., polymer-supported chromic acid, osmium tetroxyde, fluoride ion, chlorine, bromine, and so on. Several of these reagents are present in Fluka and Aldrich catalogues, and some of them, particularly the polymer-supported fluoride ion, are now extensively used.

Recently, effects of the solvent and temperature on the selectivity have been under investigation.

The importance of the solvation and the temperature, as well as the paramount importance of the activation entropy on the diastereoselectivity of a number of completely different reactions including enzymatic reactions, has been demonstrated. It has been shown that for any reagent in solution, the reacting species is not the molecule as such, as it occurs in vacuum, but it is present in a rather well-defined solute-solvent cluster that behaves like an independent chemical species. Very often, two such solute-solvent clusters are present in equilibrium at a temperature called inversion temperature so that, depending on the temperature and the nature of the solvent, the same molecule behaves like two different chemical species. This very interesting topic is actively investigated in Cainelli's group (*Angew. Chem. Int. Ed.* **2000**, *39*, 523).

Tagliatelle alla Bolognese

Starting materials (serves 4):

Pasta:

400 g flour

pinch of salt

4 eggs

water

Sauce:

200 g peeled tomatoes

200 g minced meat

1 onion (not too large)

1 carrot

1 stalk of celery

5 tbsp white whine

extra virgin olive oil

salt, pepper

To make the pasta :

Knead 400 g flour, a pinch of salt, and 4 eggs with sufficient water to form a firm, smooth dough. Flour a worktop and, using a rolling pin and pasta maker, roll out until very tin. Roll up and cut into 10-mm wide strips of tagliatelle that should be as long as possible.

To make the sauce (ragù)

Concerning the meat, beef prevails, but also veal, pork, or turkey, and pancetta can be used.

Fry the finely chopped onion, carrot, and celery in a few tbsp of olive oil until brown.
Browning is the taste foundation of the ragù. Slow browning over low heat brings out the sweetness of the onion and carrot, while fast browning over high heat yields punchier, more robust flavors. Browning on medium heat strikes a balance between the two and is preferable.
Once the onion begins to color, add the meat. Beef is often used by itself in Bologna, although it is frequently blended with veal, pork, turkey, and pancetta. After a few minutes pour in the wine. When evaporated, add the chopped tomatoes and season with salt and pepper. Cook over moderate heat for at least 2 hours.
Cook tagliatelle in plently of hot, salted water until "al dente" (in general, no more than 5 min). Drain tagliatelle, add the ragù, and serve with freshly grated parmesan cheese. Some people prefer the dish without.

«In Bologna alone, you will find hundreds
of variations on the theme of ragù.»

«Tagliatelle are noodles about 10 mm wide. If the noodles are 5 mm wide,
they are called fettuccine. Fettuccine are used in southern Italy, especially in
Rome, but in northern Italy, and particularly in Bologna, the tagliatelle are
much more common. The people of Bologna maintain that they are good
only if they are prepared completely by hand, and all women, including most
of the young ones, are capable of preparing tagliatelle using the rolling pin
with masterly skill.»

Gianfranco Cainelli

Erick M. Carreira

was born in Havana, Cuba, in 1963. He earned a B.S. degree in 1984 from the University of Illinois at Urbana-Champaign under the supervision of S. E. Denmark and a Ph.D. degree in 1990 from Harvard University under the supervision of D. A. Evans. After carrying out postdoctoral work with Peter Dervan at the California Institute of Technology through late 1992, he joined the faculty at the same institution as an assistant professor of chemistry and subsequently was promoted to the rank of associate professor of chemistry in spring 1996 and full professor in spring 1997. Since September 1998, he has been full professor of Organic Chemistry at the ETH Zürich. He is the recipient of the American Chemical Society Award in Pure Chemistry, the Nobel Laureate Signature Award, the Fresenius Award, a David and Lucile Packard Foundation Fellowship in Science, the Alfred P. Sloan Fellowship, the Camille and Henry Dreyfus Teacher Scholar Award, the Merck Young Investigator Award, the Eli Lilly Young Investigator Award, the Pfizer Research Award, the National Science Foundation CAREER Award, the Arnold and Mabel Beckman Young Investigator Award, and a Camille and Henry Dreyfus New Faculty Award. He is also the recipient of the Associated Students of the California Institute of Technology Annual Award in Teaching and a Richard M. Badger Award in Teaching.

Scientific Sketch

Carreira's research program focuses on the asymmetric synthesis of biologically active, stereochemically complex natural products.

Target molecules such as epothilone B (Fig. 1) are selected that pose unique challenges in asymmetric bond construction (*J. Am. Chem. Soc.* **2001**, *123*, 3611).

Figure 1. Epothilone B.

These asymmetric bond formations require new synthetic methodologies; another important field of research in Carreira's group is the development of these methods.

Drawing from the areas of organometallic chemistry, coordination chemistry, and molecular recognition, Carreira's group is developing catalytic and stoichiometric reagents for asymmetric stereocontrol, including chiral *Lewis* acids.

The asymmetric addition of terminal alkynes to aldehydes (Fig. 2) catalyzed by chiral zinc complexes is a useful tool for the preparation of chiral building blocks in natural product synthesis (*J. Am. Chem. Soc.* **2000**, *122*, 1806).

R= ^{i}Pr : 95% (96% *ee*)
R= cy : 88% (97% *ee*)
R= Ph : 57% (97% *ee*)

Figure 2. Asymmetric addition of alkynes to aldehydes.

Another powerful reaction is the transition metal-catalyzed aldol addition of silyl enol ethers, silyl ketene acetals, and dienolates to aldehydes. Catalysts for these transformations have been developed in Carreira's group (Fig. 3).

R = Ph : 96% *ee*
R = propyl : 95% *ee*
R = cinnamyl : 97% *ee*

Carreira's catalyst

Figure 3. Asymmetric addition of ketene acetals to aldehydes.

Starting with Ti(IV)-complexes (Carreira's catalyst, Fig. **3**, *J. Am. Chem. Soc.* **1994**, *116*, 8837), new copper catalysts have been synthesized recently that are highly reactive and selective (Fig. 4, *J. Am. Chem. Soc.* **1998**, *120*, 837).

R = Ph : 94% *ee*
R = 2-Thienyl : 95% *ee*
R = 2-Naphtyl : 93% *ee*

Figure 4. Asymmetric dienolate additions.

Black Bean Soup

Starting materials:

450 g dried black beans

1 bay leaf

2 medium-sized green bell peppers, seeded and cut into small pieces

175 mL olive oil

4 cloves garlic, finely chopped

2 large onions

3 tsp ground cumin

1 tbsp oregano

2 tbsp cider vinegar

2 beef bouillon cubes

The black beans should be washed with cold water, and any beans that float to the top or are discolored should be removed and disposed of. The beans should be soaked overnight in cold water to cover 4 cm. The next day the water should be thrown away and the beans washed again with cold water. The beans are now ready for cooking. After covering with water by 5 cm, the bay leaf is added before bringing the beans to a boil over high heat. The heat can be reduced to low and the beans cooked until they are tender and almost cracked open, 2–3 hours depending on the quality and freshness of the beans. If a pressure cooker is used, this requires only 15 minutes of cooking at full pressure. The beans should be checked during the cooking, and more water can be added as needed.

As the cooking of the beans nears completion, the sofrito can be prepared. In a frying pan the olive oil is heated over low heat and then the garlic, onion, and bell pepper are added. This mixture is cooked with stirring until the onion is semi-transparent, approximately 10 minutes. The cumin and oregano are subsequently added and thoroughly mixed in.

The sofrito is added to the beans along with the beef bouillon cubes and vinegar. The mixture is thoroughly mixed and cooked over low heat covered for an additional 30–40 minutes until the beans crack open. Prior to serving, salt can be added to taste. The black bean soup can be eaten as a soup or alternatively over white rice.

«I was born in Cuba; thus this recipe is a family one.»

Erick M. Carreira

Armin de Meijere

was born in 1939 in Homberg (Niederrhein), Germany. He studied chemistry at the universities of Freiburg and Göttingen, and obtained his doctoral degree (Dr. rer. nat.) in 1966 at the University of Göttingen under the guidance of W. Lüttke. Following postdoctoral training under K. B. Wiberg at Yale University, he fulfilled the requirements for his habilitation in 1971 at the University of Göttingen. He became full professor of organic chemistry at the University of Hamburg in 1977 and returned to the University of Göttingen to succeed his former mentor as the Chair of Organic Chemistry in October 1989. He has been visiting professor at the University of Wisconsin, Madison; the IBM Research Laboratory in San José, California; the Technion in Haifa, Israel; Princeton University, New Jersey; the Université de Aix-Marseille III, France; the Università degli Studi, Firenze, Italy; the École Normale Supérieur, Paris, France; the University of Colorado; and the University of Florida. He received a fellowship from the Studienstiftung des Deutschen Volkes and earned the award "Dozentenstipendium" from the Fonds der Chemischen Industrie in 1972. He was elected a member of the Norwegian Academy of Sciences and Letters in 1992, and in 1996 he received the Alexander von Humboldt Gay Lussac Prize of the French Ministry for Higher Education and Research. In 1997 he was elected as a member of the Braunschweigische Wissenschaftliche Gesellschaft and as an Honorary Professor of the St. Petersburg State University in St. Petersburg, Russia, and nominated as a Fellow of the Japan Society for the Promotion of Science. In 1999 he was granted a Lady Davis Visiting Professorship at the Technion in Haifa, Israel. He is editor or member of the editorial board of a number of scientific journals, including *Chemical Reviews, Chemistry – A European Journal, Synlett*, periodicals such as *Topics in Current Chemistry, Houben-Weyl*, and other books. His scientific achievements have been published in more than 500 original publications, review articles, and book chapters.

Scientific Sketch

The research interests of Armin de Meijere continue to have their focus on various aspects of small-ring chemistry as well as organometallic complexes and transformations.

Some recent highlights of theoretically interesting molecules are the third-generation bicyclopropylidene (1) (*Chem. Eur. J.* **2001**, *7*, 4021), the enantiomerically pure [5]triangulane (2) (*Chem. Eur. J.* **2002**, *8*, 828), and the decacyclopropylferrocene (3) (*Angew. Chem.* **2002**, *114*, 811).

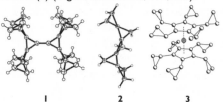

1	2	3

Among the newly developed synthetically useful building blocks, methyl 2-chloro-2-cyclopropylideneacetate (4) (*Top. Curr. Chem.* **2000**, *207*, 149) and bicyclopropylidene (5) (*Top. Curr. Chem.* **2000**, *207*, 89) are the front runners. Various dinucleophiles react with 4 to form heterocycles, e.g., carboxamides and thiocarboxamides yield spirocyclopropanated oxazolinecarboxylates (6) and thiazolinecarboxylates (7). The phenyl derivative 6 (R = Ph) has been used to prepare a paclitaxel (Taxol®) analogue with a cyclopropanated side chain (*Tetrahedron Lett.* **2003**, submitted), and the hydrolysis of 7 yields a cyclopropanated analogue of penicillamine. Bicyclopropylidene (5) undergoes carbopalladation more rapidly than methyl acrylate. Thus, 5 is the key partner in a new one-pot three-component reaction incorporating an aryl iodide and a dienophile to give high yields of spiro[2.5]octene derivatives (8) (*Top. Curr. Chem.* **2000**, *207*, 89).

The titanium-mediated reductive cyclopropanation of *N,N*-dialkylcarboxamides (9) with *Grignard* reagents, known as the *de Meijere-Kulinkovich* reaction, provides an easy access to *N,N*-dialkylcyclopropylamines (10) (*Titanium and Zirconium in Organic Synthesis* (ed.: I. Marek), Wiley-VCH, Weinheim, **2002**, p. 390). Functionally substituted cyclopropylamines such as 11 (*Org. Synth.*

2003, *80*, in press) and the orthogonally bisprotected bicyclic diamine (12), a versatile scaffold for various pharmacophores (*Chem. Eur. J.* **2002**, *8*, 3789), are thus easily obtained.

Metal-catalyzed and metal-assisted cascade reactions constitute the other domain of de Meijere's research activities. For example, the palladium-catalyzed tetracyclization of 2-bromodieneynes (13a,b) forming four new C-C bonds, occurs with remarkable efficiency (74–76% yield of 14a,b) and complete diastereoselectivity.

This methodology has led to the construction of the tetracyclic analogue of the steroid skeleton 15 (*J. Organomet. Chem.* **1999**, *576*, 88). 3-Dialkylamino-substituted α,β-unsaturated *Fischer* carbene complexes like 16 have established themselves as chemical multitalents (*Angew. Chem. Int. Ed.* **2000**, *22*, 3964).

The enantiomerically pure terminal alkyne 16, prepared from (+)-2-carene, was converted in a one-pot operation to the carbene complex 17 (84%). Insertion of 2-butyne with cyclization gave the cyclopentadiene 18 (72%), which, upon consecutive treatment with acid and then base, furnished the enantiomerically pure triquinanedione (19) in 60% yield (*Synlett* **2002**, 875).

Spaghetti con "Schluntz"

**Starting materials
(serves 4):**

600 g chopped meat (50%
pork, 50% beef)

4–5 medium-sized onions

100 g bacon fat

50 g tomato concentrate

50–100 g tomato ketchup

salt, pepper, paprika powder
(sweet and hot)

400 g spaghetti

The procedure

In a large enough frying pan, heat the finely cut bacon fat until the cubicles start to turn yellow, add the finely cut onions, and fry the mixture with vigorous stirring until the onion pieces start to turn light brown. Add the chopped meat and keep frying. To avoid clogging, keep pressing and stirring the mixture with a flatly held large fork. When the meat is well done, add the tomato concentrate and ketchup as desired. Also add seasonings to taste with stirring and mixing. For a hotter variety, Tabasco sauce may be added. If necessary, add some water to attain the desired consistency (it should be neither too liquid nor too thick, more like a paste).

Cook spaghetti in boiling, slightly salted water "al dente." Serve with "Schluntz" while still hot.

«This recipe dates back to my early student years, and in late May of 1960, I was even able with this main course to impress my then-new girlfriend Ute Fitzner, who four years later became my wife. One may also consider this protocol as an early example of the "combinatorial kitchen", since all ingredients may be varied in their ratio so that the corresponding product will be obtained with vastly differing taste. Thus, the given quantities will assemble only one example of a whole library of taste profiles.»

Armin de Meijere

Scott E. Denmark

was born in New York on June 17, 1953. He obtained an S.B. degree from the Massachusetts Institute of Technology in 1975. His graduate studies were carried out at the Eidgenössische Technische Hochschule (ETH) in Zürich under the direction of A. Eschenmoser and culminated with the D. Sc. Tech. degree in 1980. That same year he began his career as assistant professor at the University of Illinois. He was promoted to associate professor in 1986 and to full professor in 1987 and then in 1991 was named the Reynold C. Fuson Professor of Chemistry.

Scott Denmark has won a number of honors for both research and teaching. These include the Eli Lilly Research Award, the Beckman Endowment Research Award, an A. P. Sloan Foundation Fellowship, the NSF Presidential Young Investigator Award, the Procter and Gamble University Exploratory Research Program Award, the University Scholar (University of Illinois), the School of Chemical Sciences Teaching Award, the Stuart Pharmaceuticals Award, the Arthur C. Cope Scholar Award, the Alexander von Humboldt Senior Scientist Award, the Pedler Lecturership (Royal Society of Chemistry), and the ACS Award for Creative Work in Synthetic Organic Chemistry. Furthermore, he is a Fellow of the American Association for the Advancement of Science. Professor Denmark is currently a member of the Board of Editors of *Organic Reactions* and *Organic Syntheses* and has served on many editorial advisory boards. He is an Associate Editor of *Organic Letters* and the *Encyclopedia of Reagents for Organic Synthesis*. He is also the Editor of *Topics in Stereochemistry*.

Scientific Sketch

Scott E. Denmark is primarily interested in the invention of new synthetic reactions and the elucidation of the origin of stereocontrol in fundamental carbon-carbon bond-forming reactions. He has carried out extensive mechanistic and stereochemical studies on the additions of allylmetals to aldehydes and acetals and has investigated the origins of stereocontrol in aldol reactions. The current emphasis in his laboratories centers on the relationship among structure, reactivity, and stereoselectivity in a variety of organo-element systems.

He demonstrated the stereocontrolled construction of 9-, 10-, 11-, and 12-membered rings containing a 1,3-*cis-cis* diene unit via an intramolecular silicon-assisted, palladium-catalyzed, cross-coupling reaction (Fig. 1, *J. Am. Chem. Soc.* **2002**, *124*, 2102).

Figure 1. Intramolecular silicon-assisted cross-coupling reaction.

Denmark and coworkers are also interested in the asymmetric catalysis of aldol and allylmetal addition reactions with chiral *Lewis* bases. In addition to the *Lewis* base activation in additions of silyl enol ethers and ketene acetals to aldehydes (*J. Am. Chem. Soc.* **2002**, *124*, 13405; *Acc. Chem. Res.* **2000**, *33*, 432), Denmark also studies the catalytic, enantioselective aldol addition to ketones with chiral *Lewis* bases (Fig. 2, *J. Am. Chem. Soc.* **2002**, *124*, 4233).

Figure 2. Catalyzed addition of silyl ketene acetals to ketones.

Asymmetric reactions of dioxirane-based oxidizing agents are developed and investigated for the catalytic enantioselective epoxidation of alkenes (Fig. 3, *Synlett* **1999**, 847).

Figure 3. Catalytic, enantioselective epoxidation of alkenes with chiral nonracemic dioxiranes.

Futhermore, his research program encompasses the development and application of tandem heterodiene cycloadditions for the synthesis of complex polycyclic nitrogen-containing compounds, such as *all-cis*-[5.5.5.5]-1-azafenestrane (Fig. 4, *Angew. Chem. Int. Ed.* **2002**, *41*, 4122).

Figure 4. Synthesis of [5.5.5.5]-1-azafenestrane.

Scott's Fondue

Starting materials for each hungry person:

250 g grated cheese
(100 g Gruyère,
50 g Vacherin,
50 g Appenzeller,
50 g Tilsiter, for a stronger tasting fondue, use less Vacherin and more Appenzeller).

125–175 mL dry white table wine, or for a festive touch … champagne

1 small clove garlic

1 tsp corn starch (cream of tartar)

50 mL Kirsch, not to sweet

freshly ground black pepper

dense bread (St. Gallen style), baguette will do if necessary, cut into 40 mm cubes.

In a cast iron, enameled fondue pot, press the garlic into the wine and bring to a rolling boil. Add the grated cheese portionwise, stirring with a whisk and waiting for the cheese to dissolve before each additional portion.

When all the cheese is added, stir over medium heat in a rapid figure eight until the cheese/wine mixture is smooth (ca. 5 minutes).

Mix the corn starch into the Kirsch and pour the mixture into the cheese, whisking continuously. Stir the mixture vigorously over medium heat until the desired consistency results. Add freshly ground pepper and transfer to a heated plate or fondue burner. Impale a piece of bread on a long fork and submerge with stirring into the cheese mixture.

«There is plenty of Swiss lore about the consequences of losing your bread in the cheese, but, depending upon the company, you can make up your own rules!»

Scott E. Denmark

Ulf Diederichsen

was born on October 7, 1963 in Munich and started his chemistry studies in 1983 at the University of Freiburg/Brsg. In 1988 he graduated under the guidance of H.-J. Gais. Afterwards he went to A. Eschenmoser at the ETH Zürich where he obtained his Ph.D. in 1993 with a thesis about base-pairing properties of hypoxanthine in HOMO-DNA oligonucleotides and of glycopyranosyl-oligonucleotides. A following postdoctoral stay led him to D. P. Curran at the University of Pittsburgh, from where he came back in 1994 to finish his habilitation in 1999 at the Technical University of Munich. He became associate professor at the University of Würzburg in the same year and accepted a chair as full professor at the Georg-August-University Göttingen in 2001.

During his short career until now, Diederichsen has received the Award of the Hellmut-Bredereck Foundation and a Karl Winnacker Grant. He was visiting professor at the LMU München and the University of Wisconsin in Madison in 2000 and is currently a member of the advisory board of *Molecules*. Together with T. Lindhorst, B. Westermann, and L. A. Wessjohann, he is editor of the monograph *Bioorganic Chemistry* (Wiley-VCH, 1999).

Scientific Sketch

A major part of Diederichsen's research is focused on alanyl-PNA. This artificial biooligomer is based on a regular peptide backbone and nucleobases attached to the amino acid side chains. Because of its structural rigidity and well-defined base pair orientations, alanyl-PNA is usefull as a DNA model. Intercalation, artificial base pairing, base-pair-mediated electron transfer, and hydration can be studied in detail (Fig. 1).

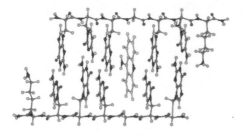

Figure 1. Intercalation of aminoacridine to alanyl-PNA.

Stable secondary structures such as extended strands or helices can be obtained by alanyl-PNA as well as by peptides based on homologues of β-nucleo amino acids. These secondary structures can be organized by base pair recognition in order to mimic biological systems such as the i-motif tetrade or helix bundles (Fig. 2).

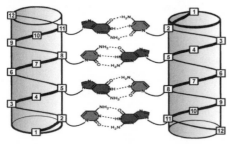

Figure 2. β-Peptide helices organized by nucleobase pairing.

Incorporation of alanyl-PNA in proteins using native chemical ligation is a promising tool for conformational switching of the protein structure. In DNA chemistry, the conformational control of the Z-DNA is a target in order to look for selective Z-DNA binders and to understand protein regulation.

Nucleo amino acids are interesting isosters for proteinogenic amino acids. They were incorporated in peptides and proteins for improving binding stability and selectivity. Further, nucleobase containing triostin analogues were prepared as potential DNA bisintercalators (Fig. 3).

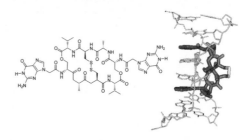

Figure 3. Triostin A bisintercalating in DNA and its nucleobase modified analogue.

Green Eel à la Marie with Dill Dip

Starting materials (serves 4):

4 eels (approx. 300 g each)

¾ L water

½ tsp salt

2 bay leaves

2 chopped onions

2 tbsp chopped parsley

2 tbsp chopped dill

1 tsp pepper

a pinch of sugar

1 tbsp sauce thickener or starch

1 tbsp lemon juice

1 bunch of dill

butter

Remove the innards, fins, and heads of the eel and rinse under cool running water, if necessary, pat dry, and cut into 6-cm sections.

Add the salt, the bay leaves, the chopped onion, the chopped herbs, some ground pepper, and the sugar. Do not add the lemon juice at this stage because this might make the fish hard. Add the eel pieces and simmer for about 20 minutes until cooked (this can be controlled by spearing).

Bind the sauce with thickener, and add the lemon juice and the chopped dill. Cover with butter flakes. Optionally, the sauce can be refined by adding some crème fraîche.

We serve this dish preferably with cucumber salad (also with dill) and with steamed potatoes, of course.

«This recipe was taken from A. Sievers, Das Fisch-Fiete Fisch-Kochbuch, Heyne, München, 1986. If you prepare everything correctly – during my first trial I forgot to remove the gall-bladder... – this recipe is almost as delicious as the original at the fish-restaurant "Fisch-Fiete" in Keitum/Sylt.»

Ulf Diederichsen

Alessandro Dondoni

has been Professor of Organic Chemistry at the University of Ferrara since 1975. Before that he was at the University of Bologna where he started his academic career, first as assistant professor and then as associate professor. He has held visiting professorships at the University of Rennes (1982), the University of Hamburg (1983), the University of Osaka (1988, JSPS Award), and the University of Lyon (1994). He was awarded the 1996 A. Mangini Gold Medal by the Italian Chemical Society for creative work in heterocyclic chemistry. In 1999 he earned the Avogadro-Minakata Lectureship Award of the Chemical Society of Japan and the Ziegler-Natta Lectureship Award of the German Chemical Society. In the same year, he received the Italian Minister of Cultural Heritage and Activities Prize in Chemistry sponsored by Lincei National Academy. He has been elected (2002) President of the International Society of Heterocyclic Chemistry. Dondoni belongs to the Honorary Advisory Boards of several scientific journals, including *Tetrahedron Letters*, *Tetrahedron*, *Synthesis*, and the *Journal of the Chemical Society, Perkin Transactions 1*.

Scientific Sketch

While the earlier scientific activity of Dondoni dealt with studies in physical organic chemistry, such as the kinetics and mechanism of organic reactions (S- and N-oxidations, 1,3-dipolar cycloadditions), more recent work has been focused on the design and preparation of new reagents and their application in methodologies for the synthesis of natural and unnatural products. Dondoni has highlighted the synthetic equivalence of the thiazole ring to the formyl group by preparing new thiazole-based reagents that proved to be useful equivalents of various anionic synthons (Fig. 1, *Synthesis* 1998, 1681).

Figure 1. Thiazole-based reagents and their corresponding synthons.

Noteworthy is 2-trimethysilylthiazole (2-TST), a formyl carbanion equivalent stable at room temperature. This reagent has been employed *inter alia* for the iterative one-carbon chain elongation of sugar aldehydes as shown by the stereoselective homologization of D-glyceraldehyde to the various one-carbon higher homologues up to the nine-carbon-atom derivative. (Fig. 2, *Angew. Chem. Int. Ed.* 1986, 25, 835; *J. Org. Chem.* 1989, 54, 693).

Figure 2. Homologization of D-glyceraldehyde.

More complex sugar derivatives, such as the 3-desoxy-2-ulosonic acids DAH, KDO, KDN, and iso-Neu4Ac (Fig. 3), have been prepared by the use of 2-acetylthiazole (2-ATT) and the stabilized phosphorane 2-TCMP (*J. Org. Chem.* 1991,

56, 5295; *J. Am. Chem. Soc.* 1994, *116*, 3324; *Chem. Eur. J.* 1999, 5, 3562). The first total synthesis of polyoxin J is another important achievement (*J. Org. Chem.* 1997, 62, 5497) in which a furane instead of a thiazole is exploited as a functional group equivalent.

Figure 3. Preparation of 3-desoxy-2-ulosonic acids.

While maintaining profound roots in thiazole-based chemistry, the research of Dondoni's group has been continuously moving towards new targets and topics. A general goal that has been actively pursued in recent years is the development of methodologies for the preparation of carbon-linked isosteres of oligosaccharides and glycoconjugates. Complex molecular architectures mimicking natural products or acting as molecular receptors have been prepared (Fig. 4, *Chem. Eur. J.* 2001, 7, 1371; *J. Org. Chem.* 2002, 67, 4475; *J. Org. Chem.* 2002, 67, 4722).

Figure 4. (1,6)-*C*-pentasaccharide, tetraglycosylated calixarene, and crown ether glycoconjugate.

Wild Duck in Olive Oil

**Starting materials
(serves 2-3):**

1 wild duck

½ onion

1 clove garlic

1 carrot

1 stalk celery

1 bunch sage leaves

1 small twig rosemary

3 leaves laurel

1000-1500 mL olive oil
(extra virgin)

½ glass brandy or whiskey

Take a wild duck, preferably a mallard, and keep it at 5-10 °C until it becomes high (3-4 days), then carefully pluck and liberate it from all the viscera, the head, and feet. Cut into small slices the onion, the garlic, the carrots, and the celery and mix them with rosemary, sage leaves, and laurel. Place the prepared mixture of vegetables in a saucepan with the duck. Add ground black pepper, salt, and olive oil to cover the duck completely. Heat the saucepan (without cover) for 2 hours until the oil gently boils. Turn the duck two or three times during cooking. Remove the duck from the saucepan, place it in a large dish, and keep it warm. Collect the vegetables from the oil and make a sauce by squeezing them through a vegetable mill. Place the sauce in a small tureen and add some brandy or whiskey, then warm it gently to evaporate the alcohol. Serve the duck using the sauce as a dressing.

Maccheroni con salmì di lepre alla Mantovana
Macaroni with hare sauce - Mantua way

Starting materials (serves 6):

Pickled hare:

1 hare (2–2.5 kg)

1 onion

2 cloves garlic

2 carrots

1 stalk celery

1 small twig rosemary

1 bunch sage leaves

4 leaves laurel

10 black peppercorns

5 cloves

1 L red wine (Refosco)

Sauce:

80 mL olive oil

vegetables, herbs, and spices as above

80 mL white wine

200 g tomato sauce

Pasta

800 g italian macaroni (length 6 cm, diameter 1.5 cm)

100 g parmesan cheese

Take a hare that has been liberated from the skin, the viscera, and the head and keep it in a ventilated and dry room for 5 days so that it becomes high. Wash the hare under running water and then cut it into small "natural" pieces, i.e., legs, breast, etc. Place these parts in a large saucepan. Add slices of prepared vegetables (onion, garlic, carrots, celery), the herbs (rosemary, sage leaves, and laurel), the spices (black peppercorn and cloves), and cover everything with old red wine. Keep the mixture at room temperature (20–25 °C) overnight (at least 12 hours). Take out the pieces of meat, place them in another saucepan or a roasting tin, and heat them gently for 5–10 minutes while turning the pieces of meat with a wooden spoon. Place the meat in a saucepan with the olive oil, fresh vegetables, herbs, and spices as described above and season with some salt. Add some white wine and braise uncovered until the alcohol has evaporated. Add the tomato sauce and some water to cover the pieces of meat. Heat gently and keep partially covered so that only a partial evaporation of the liquid can occur. The cooking may take two or three hours depending on the age and size of the hare. It is complete when the meat can be easily separated from the bones.

Take out the pieces of meat from the saucepan and separate the meat from the bones. Squeeze the remaining mixture through a vegetable mill to make a sauce and then add the hare meat cut into small pieces (use an appropriate knife or a mincing-knife). Finally, the sauce is homogenized by gentle heating.

Cook the pasta (macaroni) *al dente* in a pot containing abundant water with a little salt. Mix the hare sauce with the strained macaroni, then add abundant parmesan cheese and eventually some slices of butter. It has to be served warm.

Suggested red wines: Refosco or Cabernet Franc (at least 4 years old).

Buon appetito !

«I spent most of my childhood in the country living in a small town called Ostiglia, which is 30 km distant from the city of Mantova in Italy. Ostiglia is located on the left bank of the Po river and in those times was surrounded by ponds, marshlands, and wide fields of wheat, corn, and grass. Water, air, and soil were clean, as the word "pollution" was still unknown. Hence, the country around Ostiglia was an ideal place to host a variety of wild animals including many types of ducks in winter and quails, pheasants, and hares in summer and autumn. According to the longstanding traditions of the country life, people were used to taking advantage of these gifts from Nature. In those times fishing and hunting were natural activities which were practiced not as a sport or for pleasure but for catching some good food to eat. In general a good meal was served only on special occasions and normally on Sunday. Here are two recipes from my country which I still follow to prepare special dinners for my wife and a few selected friends. The recipes require the sacrifice of two very noble wild animals, the mallard, a superb flyer and colorful duck, and the hare, a potent runner of unequal elegance. Please enjoy the meal in good company and thank God for these marvellous gifts from Nature which He created.»

Alessandro Dondoni

Dieter Enders

was born 1946 in Butzbach, Germany. He obtained his diploma in 1972 and a Ph.D. degree in 1974 from the University of Giessen, Germany, under the guidance of D. Seebach. After a postdoctoral year at Harvard University with E. J. Corey, he returned to the University of Giessen, Germany, for his habilitation, where he was appointed lecturer in 1979. In 1980 he became associate professor at the University of Bonn, and since 1985 he has been full professor and director at the Organic Chemistry Department at the RWTH Aachen, Germany. Among his several fellowships and awards are the Heisenberg Fellowship of the Deutsche Forschungsgemeinschaft (1979-1980), the Leibniz Award of the Deutsche Forschungsgemein-schaft (1993), the Yamada Award of Japan (1995), the Max Planck Forschungspreis for Chemistry (2000), and the Emil Fischer Medal of the GDCh (2002). He is Editor in Chief of *Synthesis* and a member of the advisory boards of *Synlett* and *Tetrahedron: Asymmetry*.

Scientific Sketch

The current research interests of Dieter Enders and his coworkers are focused on the development of highly stereoselective bond construction methods, their application in the synthesis of natural products and bioactive compounds in general, and combinatorial chemistry. A number of years ago, Enders developed a general methodology for asymmetric electrophilic substitutions of aldehydes and ketones masked as chiral hydrazones. As derivatives of proline, a chiral-pool compound, these so-called "Enders-auxiliaries" are easy to prepare. Using this method, α-substituted ketones or amines for instance are readily available by 1,2-addition (Fig. 1, *Angew. Chem. Int. Ed.* **1979**, *18*, 397; *Org. Lett.* **2001**, *3*, 1575; *Tetrahedron* **2002**, *58*, 2253).

Figure 2. (–)-Callystatin A.

Another research topic is the iron-mediated allylic substitution. Chiral allylic ethers are transformed into their iron complexes: these complexes can be alkylated with several nucleophiles. This method has also been used in some total syntheses, e.g., myoporone (Fig. 3, *Synlett* **1997**, 421).

Figure 1. Asymmetric syntheses with SAMP/RAMP-hydrazones.

In many total syntheses of natural products, this asymmetric methodology has been used, e.g., (–)-callystatin A has been synthesized in this research group (Fig. **2**, *Chem. Eur. J.* **2002**, *8*, 4272).

Figure 3. Iron-mediated allylic substitution.

Enders is also engaged in asymmetric catalysis employing nucleophilic carbenes. Further current projects involve metalated aminonitriles, silylated ketones, lactams, sulfonamides, and sulfonates.

Chicken à la Maritje

Starting materials (serves 4):

3 tbsp oil

1 onion

100 g mushrooms

500 g chicken filets

125 mL soy sauce or ketjap Manis

250 mL water

125 mL chopped tomatoes or tomato sauce

1 tsp Sambal Oelek

2 tsp brown sugar

1 tbsp balsamic vinegar

1 tsp starch

Heat the oil in a large pan or skillet. Chop onions, slice mushrooms, and cut chicken into serving pieces. Sauté onions, and add the mushrooms and chicken pieces. Fry them until golden brown on all sides. Add remaining ingredients and simmer, stirring, 10 minutes. Stir in the starch dissolved in water or ketchup, reduce the heat, and simmer stirring constantly until thickened.

Serve with rice and a crisp green salad.

«Maritje is the wife of a Dutch mathematician who was a post-doc at Harvard University in Cambridge, Massachusetts, at the same time as myself. We got the recipe from her: we love it – so do my kids.»

Dieter Enders

David A. Evans

was born in Washington D.C. in 1941. He received his A.B. degree
from Oberlin College in 1963 and he obtained his Ph.D. at the California Institute of Technology in 1967, where he worked under the
direction of R. E. Ireland. In that year he joined the faculty at the
University of California, Los Angeles. In 1973 he was promoted to
the rank of full professor and shortly thereafter returned to Caltech
where he remained until 1983. In 1983 he joined the Faculty at Harvard University, and in 1990 he was appointed as Abbott and James
Lawrence Professor of Chemistry. Presently, he is serving as the
Chairman of the Department of Chemistry and Chemical Biology.
Evans is the recipient of a Camille and Henry Dreyfus Teacher-
Scholar Award (1971), an A. P. Sloan Fellowship (1972), a Distinguished Teaching Award, UCLA (1973), the American Chemical
Society Award for Creative Work in Synthetic Organic Chemistry
(1982), and the Arthur C. Cope Scholar Award (1988). He was
elected to the National Academy of Sciences in 1984 and the
American Academy of Arts and Sciences in 1988.

Scientific Sketch

Evans has made fundamental advances in the design of stereoselective reactions and the application of these reactions to natural product synthesis. Over the last two decades, reaction methodology directed towards achieving absolute stereocontrol in carbon-carbon bond-forming reactions has been one of the central topics that have been developed in his laboratory.

In the early 1980s the diastereoselective addition of chiral enolates to aldehydes was developed by Evans and coworkers (Fig. 1, *J. Am. Chem. Soc.* **1981**, *103*, 2127).

R = Ph : 89 %, *dr* > 500 : 1
R = *i*Bu : 78 %, *dr*   497 : 1

Figure 1.   Diastereoselective addition of enolates to aldehydes.

Using chiral-pool auxiliaries, this reaction is not limited to aldol additions: chiral enolates can also be alkylated with several electrophiles (Fig. 2).

R = H₂C=CHCH₂ : 78 %, *dr*   99 : 1
R = PhCH₂   : 78 %, *dr* > 99 : 1

Figure 2. Alkylation of chiral enolates.

This synthetic method has been established in the total synthesis of several natural products such as discodermolide (Fig. 3) and is known as the *Evans* aldol reaction (*Evans*-alkylation).

Figure 3. Discodermolide.

A more recent synthetic aspect is developing chiral catalysts for enantioselective catalysis: copper bisoxazoline complexes catalyze the enantioselective addition of silylthioketene-acetals to benzyloxyacetaldehyde in high yields and with excellent enantioselectivity (Fig. 4, *J. Am. Chem. Soc.* **1997**, *119*, 7893).

96 %
99 % ee

catalyst

Figure 4. Enantioselective addition of silylketeneacetals.

Such complexes catalyze a great variety of organic transformations: depending on the metal (e.g., Cu, Sn), the oxidation state, and the counter-ion (OTf, Cl, SBF₆), many transformations are catalyzed, e.g., *Diels-Alder* reactions, cyclopropanations, and *Michael*-additions.

Brunswick Stew (Lonely Soup)

Starting materials (serves 4):

1 large chicken

4–5 stalks celery-chopped

1 large onion-chopped

1 large can (900 g) crushed tomatoes

1 large package frozen corn

1 small can (200 g) creamed corn

1 large package frozen baby lima beans

2 tsp sugar and salt to taste

fresh ground pepper and Tabasco sauce (amount depends on who is going to eat it)

Boil one large frying chicken in ca. 1.5 qt water for 1 hour; remove, cool, and debone. In the meantime, add the ingredients listed on the left to the broth.

Gently cook the above for 3–4 hours. You may want to add some more water or some canned chicken broth to achieve the desired consistency. Add the chicken and cook for an additional hour. Skim off any fat if you were foolish enough to add the chicken skin.

This is a popular tidewater Virginia recipe given to our family by Katherine Neale, Bowler's Wharf, Va. Originally, the meat for this recipe was squirrel.

«A man can eat this recipe for 3–4 days while his wife is out of town and not get too tired of it. I now call this soup "Lonely Soup".»

«I am strictly a survival cook.»

David A. Evans

Marye Anne Fox

was born on September 12, 1947 in Canton, Ohio. She received her B.S. in 1969 at the Notre Dame College, Ohio, and her M.S. at the Cleveland State University, Ohio, in 1970. Finally, she received her Ph.D. at Dartmouth College, New Hampshire, in 1974. After a post-doctoral stay with S. L. Staley, at the University of Maryland (1974–1976), she started at the University of Texas as an assistant professor (1976–1981), then as associate professor (1981–1985), as professor (1985–1986), as Rowland Pettit Centennial Professor (1986–1991), as M. June and J. Virgil Waggoner Regents Chair in Chemistry (1991–1998), and as Vice President for Research (1994–1998). Since 1998 she has been professor and chancellor at the North Carolina State University.

She holds several honorary doctor titles and has been visiting professor at Harvard University (1989), the University of Paris VI Pierre & Marie Curie (1992), the National Science Council, Taiwan (1993), and the University of Chicago (1997). Among her numerous honors and awards are the Medal of Excellence of the American Institute of Chemists (1969), the Jean Holloway Award (1976–1977), the Alfred P. Sloan Research Fellowship (1980), the ACS Garvan Medal (1988), the Arthur C. Cope Scholar Award (1989), membership in the National Academy of Sciences (1994), the Sigma Xi Monie A. Ferst Award (1996), the New York Academy of Sciences Women of the Year Award (1999), and the honorary membership in Phi Beta Kappa (1999).

Her research is documented in more than 370 publications. She has edited and published several books, among those a famous organic chemistry textbook (with J. K. Whitesell as co-author, Jones & Bartlett, 1997). She is member of several advisory boards, including those of *Chemical Reviews* and *Organic Letters*, and the Robert A. Welch, the Camille and Henry Dreyfus, and the David and Lucille Packard Foundations.

Scientific Sketch

The research of Marye A. Fox is multidisciplinary, focusing on the relationship between structure and chemical reactivity of interesting new compounds and materials. Her group is particularly interested in controlling chemistry by photochemical or electrochemical activation.

Work is directed toward several practical goals:
1) solar energy conversion
2) environmental detoxification
3) construction of molecular electronic devices
4) synthesis and characterization of functionalized polymers
5) chemically modified surfaces for catalysis or recognition.

In one particularly fruitful area, she has investigated organic reactions on the surfaces of irradiated semiconductors and has found that controlling electron transfer in non-homogeneous media such as zeolites, thin films, or supercritical fluids is a key step (*Acc. Chem. Res.* **1999**, *32*, 201).

Fundamental to these studies is a characterization of excited states, radicals, and radical ions in these media. These studies involve not only the usual techniques of organic synthesis and mechanistic chemistry, but also special applications of laser spectroscopy, electrochemical methodology, and surface analysis (*Proc. DEO Solar Photochem. Res. Conf.* **2001**, *22*, 115; *Can. J. Chem.* **1999**, *77*, 1077).

Her group is also interested in preparing new macromolecular arrays (polymers, liquid crystals, etc.) that allow the control of macroscopic properties (such as directionality of electron transport, thermal expansion, or conductivity) in designed materials (*J. Phys. Chem.* **2001**, *105*, 10594; *ibid.* **1998**, *102*, 9820).

Design, synthesis, and characterization of functionalized self-assembled monolayers (SAMs) are becoming increasingly important as a vehicle for preparing well-ordered thin films for surface-modified nanoparticles, in order to control the mesoscopic properties of new materials and in developing new tools for nanofabrication. The Fox group reports the synthesis (*J. Org. Chem.* **1999**, *64*, 4959) and photoreactivity of several chromophores bound as a SAM at the end of a long-chain alkyl spacer bearing a terminal thiol as an anchor on a planar gold film (Fig. **1**, *J. Am Chem. Soc.* **2001**, *123*, 1464). They observed efficient photoisomerization of stilbene and photodimerization of attached stilbenes, coumarins, and anthracenes (*J. Am. Chem. Soc.* **1997**, *119*, 7211; *ibid.* **1995**, *117*, 1845).

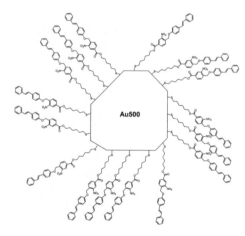

Figure 1. Schematic representation of an organic shell-metal core composite.

Carolina Dirt Cake

Starting materials:

230 g cream cheese

115 g butter

230 g freshly whipped heavy cream

1 packet (150 g) instant pudding (vanilla or chocolate)

750 mL milk

1 package cookies, crushed (Oreos, ginger snaps, or lemon crisps)

Prepare the pudding according to package directions.
Separately, mix together cream cheese, butter, and sugar. Add the thickened pudding and crushed cookies, reserving about one-third of the cookie crums for a topping. Mix thoroughly.
Pour the mixture into a loaf container, top with cookie crumbs, and refrigerate.

Burchard Franck

was born in Hamburg, Germany, in 1926. He graduated from Hamburg University with a diploma thesis on digitalis glycosides. Franck obtained his Ph.D. in organic chemistry in 1952 at the University of Göttingen, where he studied streptomyces antibiotics under the guidance of H. Brockmann. After his habilitation in 1959 in Göttingen, he accepted a chair at the University of Kiel in 1963. Six years later, he moved to Münster to become a full professor and director of the department of organic chemistry. He was visiting professor at the Massachusetts Institute of Technology, the University of Connecticut, Oslo University, as well as in Lausanne, Genf, and Fribourg in Switzerland; Guangzhum, Shanghai, and Beijing in China; and in India.

Among his numerous awards, he received the Medal of the Medical Society, Sendai, Japan (1971), the Richard Kuhn Medal of the Gesellschaft Deutscher Chemiker (1980), and the Adolf Windaus Medal of the University of Göttingen (1981). He was a member of the editorial board of *Angewandte Chemie*, *Liebigs Annalen der Chemie*, and *Heterocycles*.

Scientific Sketch

Burchard Franck (emeritus) dedicated his scientific career to natural product and bioorganic chemistry. Thus, his research group investigated the biosynthesis of porphyrins and developed the synthesis of novel porphyrinoids and macrocyclic aromatic compounds. Recently, he used porphyrins as building blocks for new aromatic 30-π-electron systems (Fig. 1, *Angew. Chem. Int. Ed.* **1997**, *36*, 2213), an analogue of octaethylporphyrine, the most widely used porphyrine in the chemical and medicinal fields.

Franck's research includes the photomedical application of porphyrines and other photosensitizers as well as the isolation, synthesis, and biosynthesis of biologically active compounds.

Due to the interest of biosynthesis of biologically active compounds, his group reported the stereoselective synthesis of tetradeuterated 1,24-dihydroxy squalene 2,3;22,23-dioxides by a double *Sharpless* epoxidation (Fig. **2**, *Tetrahedron Lett.* **1997**, *38*, 383).

Figure 2. Synthesis of precursors for the enzymatic cyclization to triterpenes.

These precursors can be transformed under enzymatic conditions into tetracyclic triterpenes, which deserve attention as possible steroid biosynthesis inhibitors.

Figure 1. Synthesis of a superaromatic 30-π-electron porphyrine.

Labskaus

Starting materials (serves 4–6):

1 kg salt meat

4 young salted hering filets

500 g onions

6 pickles

4 soused herings

500 g red beet

1 kg potatoes

20 g lard

1 bay leaf

peppercorns

1 fried egg per person

1 rollmop per person

Boil the salt meat covered with water together with bay leaf and peppercorns for approx. 1.5 hours in a closed pot so that the meat becomes slightly soft. Boil the potatoes, remove the skin afterwards, and crush them while they are still hot. Chop the onions and stew them in the hot lard until glassy, then mix them with the finely chopped or minced salt meat and the crushed potatoes. Cut the hering filets into small strips and the pickles into small cubes. Combine them with the rest. Add some meat broth if necessary. Mix the chopped red beet without its juice with the labskaus. Fill the mixture onto a preheated dish and cover with a fried egg for each person on top. Arrange the rollmops separately.

Instead of serving salt meat, one can serve corned beef, which has to be chopped and stewed together with the onions.

Labskaus

«is a typical sailor's meal, established at a time, when storage and freshness capabilities were limited on board and the smutje had the problem of preparing good-tasting meals from well-known residues. This is the reason that sharp tongues claim that sailors will retrieve everything they lost within the last year in their labskaus.»

Burchard Franck

Robin L. Garrell

Kendall N. Houk

Robin L. Garrell received her B.S. degree in biochemistry with Honors and Distinction from Cornell University in 1978 and her Ph.D. in Macromolecular Science and Engineering from the University of Michigan in 1984, where she was the recipient of Dreyfus and Lubrizol Foundation fellowships. She was an Assistant Professor at the faculty of the University of Pittsburgh until 1991, when she joined the faculty of the Department of Chemistry and Biochemistry at the University of California at Los Angeles. At UCLA, she is Co-Chair of the Materials Chemistry Interdepartmental Program, Associate Director of the Institute for Cell Mimetics in Space Exploration, a member of the UCLA NSF-IGERT Materials Creation Training Program Executive Board, and member of the Exotic Materials Institute and the Biomedical Engineering faculty. Garrell has served as President-Elect, President, and Past-President of the Society for Applied Spectroscopy (1998–2000) and as an elected member of the Coblentz Society Board of Governors (1994–1998). She is the recipient of the National Science Foundation Presidential Young Investigator Award (1985), the Herbert Newby McCoy Award for Outstanding Research at UCLA (1995), the Iota Sigma Pi Agnes Fay Morgan Award (1996), and the Hanson-Dow Award for Excellence in Teaching at UCLA (1997) and is a Fellow of the American Association for the Advancement of Science (2002).

Kendall N. Houk was born in Nashville, Tennessee, in 1943. He received his A.B. (1964), M.S. (1966), and Ph.D. (1968) degrees at Harvard University, working with R. B. Woodward. In 1968, he joined the faculty at Louisiana State University, becoming Professor in 1976. In 1980 he moved to the University of Pittsburgh and in 1986, to UCLA. Professor Houk was a Camille and Henry Dreyfus Teacher Scholar and a Fellow of the Alfred P. Sloan Foundation. He received the L.S.U. Distinguished Research Master Award in 1968, the von Humboldt U.S. Senior Scientist Award in 1981, the Akron ACS Section Award in 1984, and an Arthur C. Cope Scholar Award in 1988. He was the 1991 recipient of the ACS James Flack Norris Award in Physical Organic Chemistry and the 1998 winner of the Schrödinger Medal of the World Association of Theoretically Oriented Chemists (WATOC). He received the Bruylants Chair from the University of Louvain-la-Neuve in Belgium in 1998 and an honorary doctorate (Dr. rer. nat. h. c.) from the University of Essen in Germany in 1999. He won the Tolman Medal of the Southern California Section of the American Chemical Society in 1999. He has served on a number of Editorial Advisory Boards. From 1988 to 1990, he was Director of the Chemistry Division of the National Science Foundation. He was Chairman of the UCLA Department of Chemistry and Biochemistry from 1991 to 1994. He is a Fellow of the American Association for the Advancement of Science and of the WATOC and has been an Erskine Fellow in New Zealand, a Lady Davis Fellow and Visiting Professor at the Technion in Haifa, Israel, and a Japan Society for the Promotion of Science Fellow in Japan. He was elected to the American Academy of Arts and Sciences in 2002 and is the 2003 winner of the ACS Award for Computers in Chemistry and Pharmaceutical Research.

Scientific Sketch

Robin Garrell's research interests span analytical, materials, and biophysical chemistry. Synthesis, vibrational spectroscopy, computational chemistry, and piezoelectric methods are being used to determine mechanisms of biopolymer adhesion and molecular self-assembly on metal surfaces and to correlate molecular structure and mechanical properties in monolayers and ultrathin films.

In work on the mussel adhesive protein mefp-1, Garrell's group discovered that the DOPA and tyrosine residues in the protein's repeating decapeptide structure (Fig. 1) deprotonate and chelate to metal surfaces.

Figure 2. Schematic of EWOD-based micro-fluid chip and actual 5-μL droplet on electrode array.

Instead of pumping the liquid through channels, Garrell and her collaborators use electrical potentials to create move, cut, and join liquid droplets between two dielectric-coated arrays of electrodes using < 50 V (Fig. 3) (*J. Appl. Phys.* **2002**, 92, 4080).

Figure 1. The decapeptide repeat of *Mytilus edulis* food protein 1 (mepf-1).

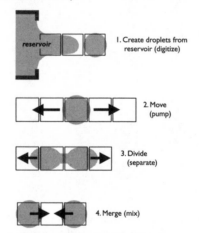

1. Create droplets from reservoir (digitize)

2. Move (pump)

3. Divide (separate)

4. Merge (mix)

Figure 3. Digitizing liquid manipulation: creating, moving, dividing, and merging.

These DOPA-metal interactions contribute significantly to the adhesive strength of the mussel protein, allowing mussels to adhere strongly to ships, pylons, and pipes (*Biopolymers (Biospectroscopy)* **2000**, 57, 92). Garrell's group is using inkjet printing technology to pattern mefp-1 and other biopolymeric adhesives to create cell arrays for artificial tissues and bioreactors.

Garrell is working with engineers to develop reconfigurable microfluid chips in which complex biological fluids can be manipulated and analyzed with very low power requirements (Fig. 2).

The surface chemistry and sequence of applied voltages are optimized to facilitate liquid motion and to minimize biomolecular adhesion. Applications of electrowetting on dielectrics (EWOD) include sensors, diagnostics, proteomics, and metabolomics.

Scientific Sketch

Kendall Houk's research involves the computational investigation of organic and biological processes, especially with the aim of determining mechanisms and the origins of stereoselectivity. Experimental research is done to test the theoretical predictions and to develop new reactions, reagents, and catalysts that have been designed from theoretical investigations.

One goal is to understand how stereoselective reactions work. Therefore, Houk and coworkers study a variety of stereoselective reactions, such as the origin of stereoselectivity in proline-catalyzed intramolecular aldol reactions of 4-alkylheptane-2,6-diones. They explored the transition states, intermediates, and geometries of these reactions using hybrid density functional theories (Fig. 1, *J. Am. Chem. Soc.* **2001**, *123*, 12911).

Figure 1. Reaction pathway of proline-catalyzed intramolecular aldolreactions.

In addition to asymmetric catalysis, Houk investigates the mechanisms of organic reactions, especially pericyclic reactions. Recently he published the application of modern theoretical methods to *Diels-Alder* and ene reactions of singlet oxygen, nitroso compounds, and triazolinediones (*Chem. Commun.* **2002**, 1243) in order to distinguish the reaction pathways (e.g., concerted or stepwise with diradical, polarized diradical, and 3-membered ring zwitterionic intermediate mechanisms).

Furthermore, the group is exploring the relationships between the structures of haptens and the corresponding antibodies produced by the immune system. Methods to calculate binding of antigens and transition states to antibodies are being developed, and experimental studies are revealing the origins of binding selectivities and catalysis by antibodies. An example is the theoretical study of the *Diels-Alder* reaction catalysis by antibody 1E9 in cooperation with D. Hilvert and coworkers (*ChemBioChem* **2000**, *1*, 255).

Houk is also interested in the field of properties and design of organic materials and devices. Thus, computational methods are applied to polyacenes and cyclacenes (Fig. 2, *J. Org. Chem.* **2001**, *66*, 5517) to calculate their geometries, electronic structures, bond equalization, vanishing band gaps, and triplet ground states.

Figure 2. Polyacene and cyclacene structures.

The chemistry and biology of nitric oxide (NO) and related nitrogen oxides and derivatives are another major principle area of Houk's research interests. After numerous electrochemical investigations and quantum mechanical calculations, Houk and coworkers reported that the reduction potential of NO is significantly more negative than it has been widely reported, which explains for the absence of NO reduction even when oxygen was reduced (*Proc. Natl. Acad. Sci. USA* **2002**, *99*, 10958).

Ahi Tuna Sashimi Napoleon

Starting materials (serves 6 as a first course):

Oil for deep frying

1 package round gyoza wrappers or wonton skins (need 18 intact for assembly)

225 g sushi-grade ahi tuna

2 tbsp mayonnaise (preferably Japanese)

2 pinches salt

1 tsp (or more, to taste) Asian chili paste with garlic

1 tsp (or more, to taste) Asian sesami oil with chili ("hot" sesame oil)

3 tbsp golden whitefish caviar or smelt eggs

whole chives for garnish (optional)

Separate the gyoza wrappers and fry to a crisp, golden brown in a deep fryer or skillet containing at least 1.5 cm oil. Try to keep the wrappers as flat as possible. Remove the wrappers from the oil, place them on paper towels, and pat dry to remove excess oil (broken or extra skins can be eaten as a snack or used to top a salad).

Mince the tuna (0.5 cm bits) with a sharp knife. Place in a bowl, add all the ingredients except the caviar or smelt eggs, and mix thoroughly. Taste for seasoning, adding more salt and chili oil as desired (it should be zesty, not painfully hot!). Gently mix in 2 tbsp of the fish eggs.

Place one wrapper on each of 6 plates. Gently spread several tablespoons of the tuna mixture on each one, so that the wrapper is covered with 1 to 1.5 cm of the filling. Top each with a second wrapper. Spread on another layer of the tuna, reserving about 2 tbsp of the tuna mixture in the bowl, and top with a third wrapper. For garnish, place a 1-tsp mound of the tuna mixture on top of each wrapper in the center and spoon on the remaining caviar.

Presentation:
Garnish each serving with two whole chives, crossed in the middle over the Napoleon. Serve with cold sake (preferably junmai), Sancerre, or a New Zealand Sauvignon Blanc.

«This is an original recipe that typifies the Asian-fusion cuisine for which California is now famous.»

Robin L. Garrell and Kendall N. Houk

Cesare Gennari

was born on April 19, 1952 in Milan where he grew up and went to school until the age of 18. He studied chemistry at the University of Milan, graduated in 1975, and worked with L. Canonica for two years. In 1978, he became assistant professor at the University of Milan in the group of C. Scolastico, from where he moved to the United States in 1982 to join the group of W. C. Still at Columbia University as a Research Associate. In 1984 he accepted an associate professorship and 10 years later a full professorship at the University of Milan.

Among numerous prestigious awards, Gennari received the Ciamician Medal of the Organic Division of the Italian Chemical Society (1986), the Federchimica Prize (1993), and the Karl Ziegler - Giulio Natta Honorary Lectureship of the Gesellschaft Deutscher Chemiker and the Società Chimica Italiana (1997). He is a member of the editorial boards of *Tetrahedron: Asymmetry* and the *European Journal of Organic Chemistry*.

Scientific Sketch

Gennari and coworkers are developing new synthetic methodologies and establishing them in synthesis of natural products and derivatives. Thus, the copper-catalyzed *Michael*-addition was investigated, and new ligands for this transformation were synthesized: these ligands are chiral *Schiff* bases and contain three metal-binding subunits, a phenol, an imine, and a secondary sulfonamide (Fig. 1, *Angew. Chem. Int. Ed.* **2000**, *39*, 916).

Figure 1. Synthesis and application of chiral tridentate ligands.

Gennari has developed a synthesis of the chiral side chain of taxol, a highly potent anti-cancer drug. Two stereogenic centers are built up in a boron-mediated aldol addition (Fig. **2**, *J. Org. Chem.* **1997**, *62*, 4746).

Figure 2. Synthesis of the taxol side chain.

With variations of this method, several isomers of the taxol side chain are available.

Recently, a strategy featuring ring-closing metathesis (RCM) as the key step was applied to the synthesis of analogues of sarcodictyin, a potent anti-cancer agent (Fig. **3**, *Tetrahedron Lett.* **2001**, *42*, 9187). The precursor dienes are accessed via a brief and efficient protocol, employing multiple stereoselective allylations. Simplified analogues retain potent tubulin-assembling and microtubule-stabilizing properties.

Figure 3. Ring-closing-metathesis approach to the sarcodictyins.

Domino Cake

Starting materials (serves 10-12):

225 g blanched almonds

225 g carrots, peeled and grated

250 mL sugar

5 eggs, separated

80 mL, plus 1 tbsp potato starch

80 mL unbleached all-purpose flour, plus extra

60 mL instant coffee

butter

confectioner's sugar

salt

Preheat the oven to 190 °C. In a food processor, grind the almonds with 1 tbsp sugar until fine. In a small bowl, whisk the yolks with 125 mL of the remaining sugar until foamy and thick. Sift the potato starch with the flour. Add the carrots, coffee, and flour mixture to the yolks and stir. Butter and flour a 20 cm springform pan. In a large bowl, beat the egg whites with a pinch of salt until soft peaks form; gradually add the remaining sugar and continue whipping until stiff. Fold the egg whites into the carrot mixture and pour the batter into the prepared pan. Bake for 1 hour, or until a cake tester inserted in the center comes out clean. Cool on a rack. Dust with confectioner's sugar.

«The cake is usually prepared by Federica (my wife) and is my favorite one. In honor of Professor Tietze, I propose to call it the "Domino cake".»

Cesare Gennari

Robert H. Grubbs

was born on February 27, 1942, near Possum Trot, Kentucky. In 1963 he received his B.S. at the University of Florida. At Columbia University he obtained his M.S. in chemistry with M. Battiste in 1965 and his Ph.D. under the guidance of R. Breslow in 1968. Between 1968 and 1969 he stayed as NIH Postdoctoral Fellow with J. P. Collman at Stanford University.

Before moving to the California Institute of Technology in Pasadena in 1978, he was associate professor at the Michigan State University (1969-1978). In 1978 he was appointed Victor and Elizabeth Atkins Professorship of Chemistry. Professor Grubbs' awards include an Alfred P. Sloan Fellowship (1974–1976), Camille and Henry Dreyfus Teacher-Scholar Award (1975–1978), an Alexander von Humboldt Fellowship (1975), the ACS Nation Award in Organometallic Chemistry (1988), the Arthur C. Cope Scholar Award (1990), the ACS Award in Polymer Chemistry (1995), the Nagoya Medal of Organic Chemistry (1997), the Fluka Reagent of the Year Award (1998), the Mack Memorial Award (1999), the Benjamin Franklin Medal in Chemistry (2000), the ACS Herman F. Mark Polymer Chemistry Award (2000), the ACS Herbert C. Brown Award for Creative Research in Synthetic Methods (2001), the ACS Arthur C. Cope Award (2002), and the ACS Award for Creative Research in Homogeneous or Heterogeneous Catalysis (2003). He was elected to the National Academy of Sciences in 1989 and to the American Academy of Arts and Sciences in 1994.

He has published more than 390 papers and more than 50 patents.

Scientific Sketch

The research group of Grubbs is involved in the design, synthesis, and mechanistic studies of complexes that catalyze organic transformations.

1   **2**

Figure 1. Catalysts for the olefin metathesis reaction.

The major focus of the group over the past few years has been on the olefin metathesis reaction. To optimize the utility of this reaction, new catalysts such as **1** and **2** have been developed that are extremely tolerant of organic functional groups (Fig. 1).

3

↓ RCM

4

Figure 2. Synthesis of complex natural products using ring-closing metathesis.

This family of ruthenium catalysts is being used in a wide range of applications in organic synthesis. The ring-closing metathesis (RCM) is one of the most used applications of these catalysts. Rings of small to medium size can be formed using this method; even macrocycles are formed if high dilution is applied. Complex natural products such as **4** (Fig. 2) can be synthesized employing these ligands.

The cross-metathesis (CM) is another useful application of the *Grubbs*-catalysts. Two different alkenes are connected to form internal, mostly *E*-configured double bonds with the loss of an alkene as propene or ethylene (Fig. 3).

Figure 3. The cross-metathesis reaction.

When cyclic alkenes are used in metathesis reactions, interesting new polymers can be synthesized (Fig. 4). The *Grubbs*-catalyst converts dicyclopentadiene into a polymer with interesting properties. This type of reaction is known as the ring-opening metathesis (ROMP)

Figure 4. The ring-opening metathesis.

Pecan Pie

Starting materials:

115 g sugar

2 tbsp flour

2 eggs

175 g syrup (white is normal but also molasses can be used)

2 tbsp butter

115 g pecans (other nuts can be used)

Mix together and pour into an unbaked pie shell (or fresh crust) that contains a small lump of butter and bake at 180 °C until the filling is set.

Butter Pie Crust (1 shell)

225 g flour – (white or mix of white and whole wheat)

115 g soft butter

¼ tsp salt

2 tbsp sugar

Mix dry ingredients and work in butter until it has the consistency of corn meal. Pat the mix into pie pan evenly and firmly. Be careful that it is not too thin on the bottom or too thick at the corners.
For pies that require a cooked shell, bake 5 min at 200 °C, then turn off oven. Remove when golden brown (about 15–25 minutes).

«The major speciality growing up in the south was the dessert. The main courses were rather bland. Over the holidays, a large number of pies would be prepared. My favorite was the pecan pie. These will last for the complete holiday season and longer (I would take a few back to school in my briefcase). This is my mother's recipe.»

Robert H. Grubbs

John F. Hartwig

was born August 7, 1964 near Chicago, Illinois, and was raised in upstate New York. He received a B.A. degree in 1986 from Princeton University and a Ph.D. degree in 1990 from the University of California, Berkeley, under the collaborative direction of Robert Bergman and Richard Andersen. After an American Cancer Society postdoctoral fellowship with Stephen Lippard at the Massachusetts Institute of Technology (1990–1992), he joined Yale University in 1992, where he is now professor of chemistry.

Professor Hartwig is the recipient of the Dreyfus Foundation New Faculty Award (1992), the DuPont Young Professor Award (1993), the National Science Foundation Young Investigator Award (1994), the Union Carbide Innovative Recognition Award (1995 and 1996), an Eli Lilly Grantee (1997), an Alfred P. Sloan Research Fellow (1996–1998), the Camille Dreyfus Teacher-Scholar Award (1997), and the Arthur C. Cope Scholar Award (1998).

Scientific Sketch

Professor Hartwig's research focuses on the discovery and understanding of new reactions catalyzed by transition metal complexes. The approaches are interdisciplinary between inorganic and organic chemistry, developing new metal chemistry and its application to synthesis as well as their mechanistic studies.

Traditionally, organometallic chemistry focused predominantly on forming and cleaving carbon-carbon and carbon-hydrogen bonds. Meanwhile, the transition metal chemistry of amines, alcohols, ethers, and boranes has grown rapidly, providing major advances in the field. This will define new areas at the crossroads of inorganic, organometallic, and organic chemistry.

In that context, Hartwig´s group has developed, for example, a regiospecific rhodium-catalyzed functionalization of alkanes and polyolefins (*J. Am. Chem. Soc.* **2002**, *124*, 1164), a mild iridium-catalyzed borylation of arenes (*J. Am. Chem. Soc.* **2002**, *124*, 390), and a method for the formation of arylamines and aryl ethers from aryl halides or sulfonates (*J. Am. Chem. Soc.* **2001**, *123*, 12905).

Another goal of Hartwig´s research group is the hydroamination of olefins using transition metal catalysis. Recently, he discovered the usefullness of palladium-catalysts for the addition of aromatic and aliphatic amines to dienes and for the addition of aromatic amines to vinylarenes, with good enantioselectivity. The mechanism of the palladium-catalyzed addition of anilines to vinylarenes (Fig. 1) was revealed through the isolation of catalytic intermediates (*J. Am. Chem. Soc.* **2002**, *124*, 1166).

Figure 1. Catalytic cycle of the hydroamination of vinylarenes catalyzed by palladium-diphosphine complexes.

Moreover, Hartwig developed a simple method to convert aryl halides and ketones, malonates, and other related carbonyl compounds to α-aryl carbonyl compounds in the presence of a base and a palladium catalyst. Familiar compounds that can be generated from these products include ibuprofen, naproxin, and tamoxifen. The reaction proceeds well and in many cases with low catalyst loadings. As part of their studies to understand this process, Hartwig and coworkers have generated both O-bound and C-bound palladium enolate complexes. These complexes undergo reductive elimination of the α-aryl ketone, ester, or amide product in good yields (*J. Am. Chem. Soc.* **2001**, *123*, 5816; *ibid.* **2001**, *123*, 8410).

Sorrel Soup
Inspired by the 2001 Bürgenstock Conference

**Starting materials
(serves 4):**

3 leeks (better) or onions or
a mixture of both

4 tbsp butter

170 g sorrel (washed with
large parts of the stem
removed)

1 large boiled potato or 2
smaller ones (peeled if not
blending with a food mill)

1.2 L chicken broth

salt and white pepper to
taste

In a pot large enough to hold 2 L, sauté the leeks or onions in butter over medium heat for about 5 min. Cut the potato into four (or two if smaller) pieces and add to the pot. Add the sorrel and sauté for a few minutes until the sorrel has turned dark and wilted. Cover with the chicken broth (I made this once with water and it was not nearly as good; it's better with homemade broth) and cook for about 45 min until the potatoes are soft. With a food mill or food processor blend until smooth.

Variant of Niçoise Salad
Inspired by the 2000 IASOC meeting

**Starting materials
(serves 4):**

½ can Italian (darker) tuna
in olive oil

50 g green and calamata
olives

1 tbsp capers

2 small shallots

1 red pepper, roasted

½–1 chopped fresh tomato,
if in season

juice from half a lemon and
some zest

250 g pasta

Their version did not have any potatoes or egg, which I see in most Niçoise Salad recipes. I guess this isn't really a Niçoise Salad, but a pasta with related ingredients. I also had a similar pasta on vacation in Venice.

Simply cook 250 g radiatore or other-shaped pasta to directions. Roast the red pepper on a gas stove or under the broiler until mostly black and, after allowing to cool in a paper bag, remove the skin without rinsing with water. Pit the olives. Julia Child says you need to mix each ingredient individually with olive oil and then combine them, but I mixed the ingredients together in a bowl, breaking up the tuna, adjusted the amounts to my taste, and added a generous amount of olive oil. Serve at room temperature.

«Although conference food is usually mediocre, I thought I would include two simple recipes that were inspired by excellent dishes at chemistry conferences I've attended. The first is a soup I made after attending the Bürgenstock conference in 2001 and the second, a pasta I started making after speaking at the Ischia Advanced School of Organic Chemistry.»

John F. Hartwig

Clayton H. Heathcock

was born in 1936. He received his B.Sc. in chemistry from Abilene Christian College, Texas, in 1958. After two years in industry, he entered graduate school at the University of Colorado and finished his Ph.D. thesis about the synthesis of steroidal heterocycles in 1963 under the guidance of A. Hassner. After a one-year postdoctoral stint with G. Stork at Columbia University, Heathcock joined the faculty of the University of California at Berkeley as assistant professor. He was promoted to the rank of associate professor in 1970, became full professor in 1975, and served the Berkeley Chemistry Department as Vice Chair (1971–1976) and Chair (1986–1989). He is currently Dean of the College of Chemistry and has received several honors during his career, including National Science Foundation Predoctoral and Postdoctoral Fellowships (1961-1964), the Alfred P. Sloan Foundation Fellowship (1967–1969), the Alexander von Humboldt United States Senior Scientist Award (1978), the Ernest Guenther Award of the ACS (1986), the ACS Award for Creative Work in Organic Synthesis (1990), the Prelog Medal of the ETH (1991), and the Herbert C. Brown Award for Creative Research in Synthetic Methods (2002). He has twice been appointed Miller Research Professor at Berkeley, was the recipient of an Arthur C. Cope Scholarship (1990), and was a Centenary Lecturer of the Royal Society of Chemistry for 1996. He is a member of the American Academy of Arts and Sciences and the National Academy of Sciences. Heathcock was Chairman of the Division of Organic Chemistry of the ACS, Chairman of the Gordon Research Conference on Stereochemistry, Editor of *Organic Syntheses*, and Editor-in-Chief of the *Journal of Organic Chemistry* (1989–99). Together with A. Streitwieser he is the author of a widely-used textbook, *Introduction to Organic Chemistry* (Prentice Hall, 1998), which is currently in its fourth edition.

Scientific Sketch

Heathcock is the practitioner of conciseness in developing new strategies for assembling biologically active natural products. His work has resulted in the construction of highly complex alkaloidal ring systems and has provided breakthroughs in solving difficult stereochemical problems in the construction of C-C bonds.

His research interests are in the area of synthetic organic chemistry, both in the development of new synthetic methods and in the exploration of new strategies for the synthesis of complex molecules. In the late 1970s he began a detailed investigation of the factors that govern the stereochemical outcome of the lithium enolate aldol addition reaction. These studies pointed out a strong correlation between enolate geometry and aldol-relative configuration and led to the widespread use of the aldol addition as a tool for "acyclic stereocontrol" (Fig. 1, J. Org. Chem. 1991, 56, 2499).

In recent years his interests have moved more in the direction of multistep synthesis of complex organic molecules, usually natural products. A powerful strategy that he has been investigating is "biomimetic synthesis," in which he tries to deduce synthetic routes purely from an examination of structural relationships within a family of structurally related secondary metabolites. That is, the mere coexistence of several related structures suggests that there exists a feasible chemical pathway between the structures. On occasion, he has been able to demonstrate these pathways in the laboratory. One example of the power of this approach to synthesis was his discovery in 1990 of a spectacular cascade of reactions leading from an acyclic derivative of squalene to the pentacyclic proto-daphniphylline (Fig. 2, J. Org. Chem. 1992, 57, 2544; J. Org. Chem. 2001, 66, 450).

Figure 1. Preparation of each of the four diastereomers via aldol-addition of various enolates to acetaldehyde.

Figure 2. Biomimetic synthesis of proto-daphniphylline alkaloid starting from a squalene derivative.

His initial studies of the aldol reaction were later extended to a similar investigation of the lithium enolate *Michael*-addition reaction.

Texas Chili

Starting materials (serves 60!):

13.6 kg coarse ground beef

850 g Gebhardt´s chili powder (500 g hot, 350 g mild)

4 kg white onions (12 large)
5.8 kg tomatoes (20 large)

4 cans tomato sauce

3.6 kg bell peppers (red, yellow, and green)

1 can vegetable broth

4 bottles Samuel Adams lager

1 head garlic

8 tbsp cumin

10 tbsp salt

2 bunches fresh cilantro

Brown meat and drain. Add chopped garlic, chili powder, cumin, salt, beer, vegetable broth, and tomato sauce. Blanch tomatoes, remove skins, and add to meat mixture. Chop onions and bell peppers and add to the reaction mixture. Bring to a boil with frequent stirring. Reduce heat and simmer for 10 hours. One hour before serving, warm the chili and stir in fresh cilantro.

«For years I prepared this every fall for my research students.»

Clayton H. Heathcock

Wolfgang Anton Herrmann

was born on April 18, 1948 in Kelheim/Donau (Bavaria) and studied chemistry at the Technical University Munich from 1967 to 1971, graduating under the guidance of E. O. Fischer. In 1973 he obtained his Ph.D. under the guidance of H. Brunner at the University of Regensburg and went to P. S. Skell at the Pennsylvania State University to perform postdoctoral research. His habilitation, finished in 1978, dealt with "organometal syntheses using diazoalkanes." One year later he became associate professor at the University of Regensburg and in 1982 became full professor at the University of Frankfurt/ Main. Since 1985 he has been full professor and Director of the Institute of Inorganic Chemistry of the Technical University Munich, following E. O. Fischer. He was elected President of the Technical University Munich in 1995 and re-elected in 1999.

Among his numerous awards are the Chemistry Prize of the Göttingen Academy of Sciences (1979), the Otto-Klung Award (1982), the Leibniz Award of the Deutsche Forschungsgemeinschaft (1986), the Alexander von Humboldt Award of the French Ministry of Education (1989), the Otto-Bayer Award of the Bayer AG (1990), the Max Planck Research Award (1991), the Pino Medal (1994), the Luigi Sacconi Medal (2000) of the Società Chimica Italiana, the Wilhelm Klemm Award of the GDCh (1995), and the Werner Heisenberg Medal of the Alexander von Humboldt Foundation (2000). He is officer of the l'Ordre d'Honneur of the French President and was decorated with the German Federal Cross of Merit. He is author of some 600 publications and owner of more than 50 patents. Together with B. Cornils, he has published the books *Applied Homogenous Catalysis with Organometallic Complexes* (VCH-Wiley, 1996) and *Aqueous-Phase Organometallic Chemistry* (VCH-Wiley, 1998). He is the editor of several scientific journals and a member of the Kuratorium of *Angewandte Chemie*.

Scientific Sketch

Herrmann's research areas reach from organometallic chemistry and catalysis, including industrial processes such as the *Fischer-Tropsch* reaction, olefin-metatheses, olefin-oxidations, biphasic hydroformylation systems, and the production of isotactical polypropylene, to the formation of metal-metal multiple bonds with ligand-free transition and main group metals. Organolanthanoid complexes, water-soluble catalysts (e.g., for hydroformylation), and inorganic and organic materials are under investigation. Special attention is paid to ceramic materials, corrosion-stable layers, and polymers but also to the determination of the effects of metals (especially aluminum, bismuth, and antimony) on biological systems.

The focus of research is presently given to organometallic catalysis in industrial chemistry.

For example, a novel four-component system for the selective catalytic oxidation of terminal alcohols to the corresponding aldehydes was developed in Herrmann's group employing H_2O_2, methyltrioxorhenium(VII) (MTO), HBr and 2,2,6,6-tetramethylpiperidine-*N*-oxide (TEMPO) (Fig. 1, *J. Organomet. Chem.* **1999**, *579*, 404). MTO has proven to be the most efficient catalyst of olefin epoxidation known to date.

Due to his interests in carbene chemistry and catalytic processes, Herrmann established a carbene-ligand-based protocol for *Heck* couplings of bromo and chloro arenes in nearly quantitative yields using very small amounts (10^{-3} mol%) of palladium-carbene complexes (Fig. **2**, *Angew. Chem. Int. Ed.* **1995**, *34*, 2371).

Figure 2. Carbene-based palladium complexes for *Heck* reactions.

Similarly, the first catalytic C-F activation of arylfluorides at ambient temperature to form novel C-C bonds was reported recently by employment of nickel(0) carbene catalysts (*Angew. Chem Int. Ed.* **2001**, *40*, 3387).

The advantages of *N*-heterocyclic carbene ligands in homogenous catalytic reactions in comparison to phosphane ligands were also demonstrated in the area of olefin metathesis (e.g., patents, DE 198 1527.5 and WO 99/51344).

Figure 1. Mechanism of the MTO/HBr/TEMPO catalyzed oxidation.

Filled Trout

Starting materials:

1 trout per person

bacon or dried meat

2 tsp butter per fish

salt

pepper

The longest part of the preparation is rinsing the trouts under cold running water until they do not feel slimy any more and all blood is scrupulously removed from the inside.

Then each fish is filled with:

a) chopped "Wammerl" (the Bavarian word for bacon or dried meat)
b) warm melted butter (2 tsp per fish)
c) small amounts of salt and pepper.

Wrap the fish with aluminum foil and bake them in the preheated oven for 15–20 minutes at 170 °C (fan-assisted oven).

Serve with new potatoes (e.g., "Erna" from Bavaria), green salad, and a light white wine, e.g., an Austrian Danube-Valley "Grüner Veltiner" from the Krems area or a "Rheingau-Riesling Kabinett."

Enjoy your meal!

«Serving fish that way makes even Bavarian people enjoy it, including the President, the Vice Presidents, and the Chancellor of the Technical University of Munich.»

Wolfgang A. Herrmann

Donald Hilvert

was born in Cincinnati, Ohio, in 1956. After receiving a B.A. degree
from Brown University in 1978, he spent a year as a predoctoral
fellow at the Swiss Federal Institute of Technology (ETH) in Zürich,
Switzerland. He subsequently obtained a Ph.D. degree in 1983 from
Columbia University under the supervision of R. Breslow. Following
postdoctoral work at Rockefeller University with the late E.T. Kai-
ser, he joined the faculty of the Scripps Research Institute in La Jolla,
California, as an assistant professor. He was subsequently promoted
to associate professor in 1989 and full professor in 1994. In 1995, he
was named the Janet and W. Keith Kellogg II Professor of Chemistry
and an affiliate of the Skaggs Institute for Chemical Biology at
Scripps. Since October 1997, he has been Professor of Chemistry at
the ETH-Zürich in the Laboratorium für Organische Chemie.
Professor Hilvert's research program focuses on understanding how
enzymes work and on mimicking the properties of these remarkable
catalysts in the laboratory. These efforts have been recognized by a
number of awards, including an Alfred P. Sloan Research Fellowship
(1991–1993), the Arthur C. Cope Scholar Award (1992) from the
American Chemical Society, and the Pfizer Award in Enzyme
Chemistry (1994).

Scientific Sketch

The Hilvert group is developing strategies for creating protein molecules with tailored catalytic activities and specificities. The goal of this work is to understand, at the molecular level, the origins of the enormous rates and selectivities that enzymes achieve. Successful enzyme engineering may also provide researchers of the future with useful catalysts for a wide range of applications in chemistry and biology.

In one approach, Hilvert and his colleagues are redesigning existing protein molecules using recombinant techniques, site-selective chemical modification, and total synthesis. For example, by chemically converting serines and cysteines into selenocysteines, they have prepared artificial selenoenzymes with novel redox and hydrolytic properties (Fig. 1, Biochemistry 1995, 34, 6616). The selenium group is also a valuable probe of structure-function relationships, which can be characterized via kinetic and structural techniques such as high-field nuclear magnetic resonance spectroscopy and X-ray crystallography.

Figure 1. Redox reaction catalyzed by seleno-subtilisin.

In a complementary approach, they are exploiting the diversity and specificity of the mammalian immune system to produce monoclonal antibodies capable of catalysis (Fig. 2, Annu. Rev. Biochem. 2000, 69, 751).

With suitably designed transition state analogues, they have successfully prepared antibody catalysts for a variety of important chemical transformations, including carbon-carbon-bond forming reactions and proton transfers. Because the properties of these molecules are defined by the structure of the transition state analogue, this strategy provides a versatile route to selective protein catalysts and sheds light on the fundamental principles of catalysis.

Figure 2. Antibody-catalyzed *Diels-Alder* reaction and respective transition state analogue (box).

Finally, they are applying the tools of molecular biology and genetics to the problem of protein design (Angew. Chem. Int. Ed. 2001, 40, 3310). Specifically, they are exploring Darwinian evolution in the laboratory as a means to study and improve their first-generation antibodies and to create new proteins on a human rather than geological time scale. To date, the Hilvert group have successfully applied this approach to studies of catalytic mechanism, topological redesign of an enzyme, and *de novo* protein design.

Farfalle with Artichoke Cream Alessandro

Starting materials:

Medium sized pasta, e.g.,
farfalle or maccheroni – to
serve 4–6

1 can (400 g) artichoke
hearts in water, drained

1 container (250 g) mascarpone cheese

150 g grated Parmesan
cheese

60 mL olive oil

salt and pepper, and
Tabasco or chili powder
(optional)

Prepare, drain, and reserve pasta. In the cooking pot, coarsely shred the artichokes with a potato masher or other implement. Add all other ingredients, stir, mix in the reserved pasta, and reheat as desired. Serves 4–6.

**Starting materials for
elaborate meal:**

4–6 servings farfalle
Alessandro (see above)

1 head endive, leaves
separated and washed

1 can (250 g) hearts of palm,
drained and sliced into bite-
sized pieces

2 chicken breasts, poached
and sliced into bite-sized
pieces

snipped chives

With a few additions, this dish becomes elegant fare for entertaining. My wife arranges a striking array of shades of white against colored plates.

Keep prepared pasta warm. Fan several endive leaves across the top of each plate. Over the leaves' lower portion, heap some pasta, scatter the hearts of palm and chicken, and sprinkle the chives. If needed, adjust the endive back into its fan. Serves 6.

«This preparation is delicious and very simple. It is unusual enough to merit interest, yet, apart from the boiling of pasta, it requires only combining rather than cooking.

Where food is concerned, I consider myself a specialist: I wash up, leaving production to my family. Fortunately, though I have little instinct for cooking, even our 13-year-old son Alex and his younger brother Beto can produce an excellent meal. It was Alex who helped create the following dish, now a family favorite named after him.»

Donald Hilvert

Reinhard W. Hoffmann

was born in 1933 in Würzburg, Germany. He studied chemistry at the University of Bonn and received his Ph.D. under the guidance of B. Helferich in 1958. After a two-year postdoctoral stay at the Pennsylvania University in the research group of G. W. Brindley, he spent another postdoctoral year with G. Wittig at the University of Heidelberg. In 1964 he obtained his habilitation and moved as a lecturer to the Technische Hochschule Darmstadt three years later. He became a professor of organic chemistry at the Philipps-University of Marburg in 1970. Since 2001 he has been professor emeritus. Reinhard W. Hoffmann was visiting professor at the University of Wisconsin, the University of Bern, the University of Califorina at Berkeley, and the University of Kyoto. In 1993 he received the Liebig Medal from the Gesellschaft Deutscher Chemiker for his brilliant achievements.

Scientific Sketch

Reinhard W. Hoffmann's research interests include the development of new methods in stereoselective C-C bond formation and their application in natural product synthesis. Special attention is paid to the allylboration of chiral aldehydes, both inter- and intramolecular variants. The products with a stereodefined substitution pattern are key intermediates in the synthesis of different types of heterocycles or natural products. Hoffmann demonstrated another application of the allylboration reaction in the total synthesis of phenalamide A2 (1) (Fig. 1, *Org. Lett.* **1999**, *1*, 1713).

Figure 1. Total synthesis of phenalamide A2.

Another field of chemical research deals with the generation and application of chiral organometallic reagents and the investigation of reaction mechanisms. Hoffmann and his group developed an asymmetric synthetic pathway to generate *Grignard* reagent **2** with ca. 90% ee (Fig. 2, *Angew. Chem. Int. Ed.* **2000**, *39*, 3072), which is used as a mechanistic probe in *Grignard* additions to carbonyl compounds and in *Grignard*-substitution reactions (e.g., *J. Chem. Soc., Chem. Commun.* **2001**, 491; *J. Am. Chem. Soc.* **2002**, *124*, 4204).

Figure 2. Asymmetric synthesis of a chiral *Grignard* reagent.

Recent research activities concern the conformational design of open chain molecular backbones. Hoffmann tries to find answers to the question of whether it is possible to create flexible backbones with preferred conformations i.e., defined shape. With the avoidance of allylic 1,3-strain and the avoidance of *syn*-pentane-interactions, he succeeded in predicting the conformational behavior of compounds such as **3** and in designing backbones with a Z- or U-shape conformation, cf. **4** and **5** (Fig. **3**, *Angew. Chem. Int. Ed.* **2000**, *39*, 2054).

Figure 3. Flexible backbones with preferred conformations.

Lamb Fillets

Starting materials (serves 1):

250–300 g lamb fillets

50 g lean gammon

1 yolk

1 onion (egg-sized)

75–100 g sour cream

1 tsp soy sauce

butter

Swiss cheese

salad

white bread

Heat the oven to 250 °C. Salt the fillets and roast one side gently for 10 minutes in a pan. Cut the gammon into 4-mm cubes and put them into a bowl. Rub the onion over it and add yolk, sour cream, and soy sauce.

Take the pan from the stove and put the fillet into a casserole. Spread the stuffing with a spoon over the meat, and add some rubbed Swiss cheese and a dozen of butter fluffs with a knife. Put the casserole into the preheated oven for approximately 20 minutes. Serve the fillet on warm plates. Enjoy the meal with some sort of salad and white bread.

The contributor suggests a red wine to accompany this meal, such as a Gironde, a St. Emilion, or a Margaux.

Meal and Music

«Especially when I am alone, the "right" music belongs to this meal.
As I am a fan of the old school of jazz music, I like listening to the records of Sidney Bechet and Mezz Mezzrow from the years 1938–1943.
London's second hand shops are a good place to enlarge my own collection.»

Reinhard W. Hoffmann

Dieter Hoppe

was born in Berlin in 1941. From 1958 to 1960 he was trained as a laboratory technician in Hannover. At first he stayed at the school as an assistant teacher before starting his chemistry studies at the University of Göttingen in 1965. He received his Ph.D. in 1970 under the guidance of U. Schöllkopf with a thesis about the synthesis of amino acids employing metalated alpha-isocyano acid esters. During his habilitation, which he finished in 1977, he worked on metalated nitrogen derivatives of carbonic acid in organic synthesis – building blocks for the penicillin and cephalosporin skeletons. After a research fellowship in the group of R. B. Woodward at Harvard University, he became associate professor at the University of Göttingen in 1978 and was promoted to a full professor when he moved to Kiel in 1985. Seven years later he accepted a chair at the University of Münster.

Between 1988 and 2000 he was a member of the editorial board of *Synthesis* and obtained, among other awards, the Otto Bayer Award (1993), the Max Planck Award for International Cooperation (1999), and the Adolf von Baeyer Medal of the Gesellschaft Deutscher Chemiker (2001).

Scientific Sketch

Hoppe focuses his interests on the development of new methods in enantioselective synthesis, especially the development and synthetic application of chiral 1-oxyallyl, 1-oxybenzyl, 1-oxyalkyl, 1-thioallyl, and indenyl anions in homoaldol reactions. His field of research includes asymmetric deprotonation reactions, mediated by chiral bases such as (–)-sparteine (Fig. 1, review: *Angew. Chem. Int. Ed. Engl.* **1997**, *36*, 3283.), as well as the synthesis of dipeptide isosters and other potentially biologically active compounds, N-sulfonyl-1,3-oxazolidines as chiral templates, and their use in natural product synthesis.

1

Figure 1. (–)-Sparteine 1.

Hoppe developed various protocols for the application of lithium reagents towards different kinds of synthetic targets (i.e., Fig. 2).

Figure 2. Stereoselective synthesis of (+)-dihydromultifidene 4.

Recently he reported the successful application of his (–)-sparteine-1-mediated lithiation method in a novel intramolecular regio-, diastereo-, and enantioselective cycloallylation reaction, which furnishes 1,2-dialkenyl substituted cyclopentanes in good to excellent yields.
This method provided stereoselective access to (+)-dihydromultifidene 4 (Fig. 2, *J. Org. Chem.* **2001**, *66*, 2842).

During the search for structurally simple inhibitors of the protein phosphatases PP1 and PP2A, Hoppe and coworkers demonstrated the power of their asymmetric electrophilic formylation using N-arenesulfonyl-2-methoxy-1,3-oxazolidine (**5**) in a flexible synthesis of structurally defined 5,6,7,8-tetrahydronaphthalene-2-carboxylic acids (**8**) (Fig. 3, *Synthesis* **2000**, 1391).

Figure 3. Use of Hoppe's oxazolidine in asymmetric formylation.

Sweet and Sour Mushroom Salad

Starting materials:

1 kg mushrooms

200 mL 3% vinegar

salt

5–10 g mustard seeds

onions

cloves of garlic

plenty of dill

fresh herbs (e.g., hyssop)

Clean the mushrooms, rinse them under cold running water, and cut them into slices (approx. 3–5 mm each). Boil with 200 mL water and 1–2 g salt for 10 minutes. Filter the hot mushrooms through a kitchen sifter and store them and the brew separately.[1] For the sauce, mix the vinegar with 200 mL of the brew (or water)[2], mustard seeds, salt, and sugar, then boil shortly, remove the pot from the stove, add onion rings and cloves of garlic cut into slices, and cool down to 50 °C.

Place the boiled mushrooms in a sealable glass or plastic bowl and mix with the chopped dill and fresh herbs. Add the cold sauce and store the bowl after cooling to room temperature in the fridge. After two days the salad will be most delicious.

Important: Due to the high content of garlic, avoid close contact with fellows on the next day!

---

[1] Using the Wood Blewit or St. George's Mushroom extends the cooking time to 12–15 minutes, because these two types are sligthly toxic in a raw state.

[2] Abolish the mushroom's brew if you are using St. George's Mushrooms (strong flour flavor), Wood Blewit (strong perfume flavor), or Delicious Milk Mushroom (sligthly bitter).

A short introduction to choose the right mushrooms for this meal:

Any kind of mushroom that keeps a fairly firm consistency after boiling can be used for this recipe, e.g., the Common Field Mushroom (*Agaricus campestris*, German: Wiesenchampignon), the Horse Mushroom (*Agaricus arvensis*, Schafchampignon), the Sheep Polypore (*Albatrellus ovinus*, Schafporling)[3], *Russula paludosa*[4] (Apfeltäubling), the Bare-Toothed Russula (*Russula vesca*, Speisetäubling), the Charcoal Burner (*Russula cyanoxantha*, Frauentäubling), the Delicious Milk Mushroom (*Lactarius deliciosus*, Echter Reizker), the St. George's Mushroom (*Calocybe gambosa*, Maipilz), or the Wood Blewit (*Lepista nuda*, Violetter Rötelritterling).
It is also possible to use Chanterelle (*Cantharellus cibarius*, Pfifferling), the Boletus (*Boletus edilus*, Steinpilz), the Bay Bolete (*Boletus badius*, Maronenröhrling), Red Aspen Bolete (*Leccinum rufum*, Espen-Rotkappe) or similar species, but it would be a pity because their own delicious flavor would be drowned.

Dieter Hoppe

---

[3] This mushroom is the best choice for this recipe. It will become a green-yellowish color during cooking. Unfortunately, it has become rare in Germany, but not in Sweden.
[4] No English common name available.

Hiriyakkanavar Ila

obtained her Ph.D. in chemistry from the Indian Institute of Technology (IIT), Kanpur, in 1968 and performed postdoctoral research
work at Purdue University (1969). Later she joined the Central Drug
Research Institute, Lucknow, India (1970), as a research scientist and
married Dr. H. Junjappa (1971), an organic chemist. Both of them
moved to North Eastern Hill University, Shillong, in 1977, a new university in northeastern India, to establish a school of chemistry
there. She became professor in 1986 and at the end of 1995 joined
the Department of Chemistry at the IIT, Kanpur, as professor. Her
research activities revolve around the design and development of
new synthetic methods for biologically important molecules, especially heterocycles and domino reactions. She has visited several
countries on lecture tours. She has been Alexander von Humboldt
fellow (1984–1985, with R. Gompper, 1998, 2000, 2001, with L. F.
Tietze), Marie Curie visiting fellow (University of Cambridge 1995),
INSA exchange visitor in UK and France (1993, 1996), and visiting
professor (Spain, 1999). She is a fellow of the Indian Academy of
Science, Bangalore (FASc) and Fellow of the Indian National Science
Academy, New Delhi (FNA).

Scientific Sketch

Ila is interested in the development of new and efficient synthetic methods for heterocyclic ring systems, e.g., benzo[*b*]thiophenes, benzo[*a*]quinolizidine, and spiro[pyrrolidin-3,3'-oxindole], that form the basic structural framework of various naturally occurring alkaloids and physiologically active drugs. She developed a route to 2,3-disubstituted and fused benzo[*a*]quinolizidine-4-thiones based on a highly regioselective [3+3] ring annelation of 3,4-dihydro-6,7-dimethoxy-1-methylisoquinoline with a variety of readily accessible acyclic and cyclic β-oxodithioesters in the presence of triethylamine in refluxing benzene. The benzo[*a*]quinolizidine-4-thiones can be readily converted to the corresponding benzo[*a*]quinolizidine-4-ones (Fig. 1, *Org. Lett.* **2001**, *3*, 229).

Figure 1. Ring annelation with β-oxodithioesters.

Heterocyclic enamines such as **1** are potentially useful for the construction of polycyclic *N*-heterocycles containing 1,2-fused tetrahydroisoquinoline cores. Annelation reactions of enaminones with various one- and two-carbon electrophilic synthons have yielded direct one-pot novel convergent routes to a variety of functionalized pyrrolo-[2,1-*a*]isoquinolines and indolo-[2,1-*a*]isoquinolines (*J. Org. Chem.* **2001**, *66*, 4457).

Ila and her coworkers developed an efficient domino process to synthesize peri- and angularly-fused polycyclic aromatic and heteroaromatic frameworks. Functionalized cyclopropyl ketones undergo a domino carbocationic cyclization and provide access to a great number of polycyclic molecules (Fig. **2**, *J. Org. Chem.* **2002**, *67*, 4916).

Figure 2. Domino cyclization reaction to build up polyclic molecules.

Recently Ila's research group found a new approach for the synthesis of spiropyrrolidinyl-oxoindole alkaloids, e.g., coerulescine and horsfiline via an iodide ion-induced rearrangement of [(*N*-aziridinomethylthio)methylene]oxoindoles to the respective spiropyrroline-2-oxindole derivatives as the key step (Fig. **3**, *Org. Lett.* **2001**, *3*, 4193).

Figure 3. Iodide ion-induced rearrangement.

Domino Chicken Curry

**Starting materials
(serves 4):**

4 chicken legs

75–100 mL plain yoghurt

1 tsp garlic paste

1 tsp ginger paste

2 tbsp onion paste

75 mL tomato purée

2 tbsp cooking oil
(sunflower)

2 tbsp Indian chicken curry
powder

freshly cut coriander leaves
for garnishing

Put the chicken pieces into a Teflon-coated casserole with a glass cover. Mix ginger, garlic paste, yogurt, cooking oil, and chicken curry powder, stir well with a flat spoon, and marinate for 4–5 hours. Put the casserole on a hot plate and allow it to cook on low heat with the cover slightly open to allow water vapors to escape. Stir with a flat spoon once in a while. Allow it to cook until most of the water has evaporated and its appearance is oily. Add onion paste and continue to cook on low heat until all moisture is evaporated and the chicken pieces become soft. Add tomato purée and continue to cook for another 10 minutes until the curry has an orange/red appearance and a good flavor. Stop heating and sprinkle coriander leaves for garnishing. The curry is ready for eating with either bread or rice along with a salad.

Notes:

It is better to cut the chicken legs into pieces below thigh joint to make eight pieces since the cooking becomes easier.

Indian chicken curry powder of good brand is available in most of the Asian stores. It is a complex mixture of several spices. If you have patience you can make it and store it in a closed jar for 2–3 months, according to the following recipe:

a.	Khuskhus (white poppy seeds)	1 tsp
b.	Cumin seeds	1 tsp
c.	Fenugreek seeds	1 tsp
d.	Black mustard seeds	1 tsp
e.	Black pepper corn	1 tsp
f.	Peeled cardamon	5 pieces
g.	Cloves	8–10 pieces
h.	Cinnamon	2.5 cm piece
i.	Coriander powder	2 full tbsp
j.	Turmeric powder	2 full tbsp
k.	Red chili powder (optional)	1 tsp

Slightly roast ingredients a–h on a hot pan, cool it, and mix it with coriander, turmeric, and chili powder. Finally grind the mass into a fine powder.

For a good taste of the curry, dehydration is necessary. The curry dilution can be adjusted according to taste.

«Although I knew Lutz F. Tietze earlier through his excellent research publications, the article which attracted my attention most was "Domino Reactions in Organic Synthesis" (*Chem. Rev.* 1996, *96*, 115–136). I therefore decided to visit him as Humboldt Fellow in 1998, which was the beginning of my association with him. My three visits to his research group (1998, 2000, and 2001) proved highly fruitful and led me to initiate domino reactions and organopalladium chemistry in my own research group in India. I therefore thought it would be a nice idea to plan a domino recipe for his 60th birthday cookbook.»

Hiriyakkanavar Ila

Karl Anker Jørgensen

was born in Århus, Denmark, on June 15, 1955. He was enrolled at Århus University to study chemistry and physics in 1975. During this period his main interest was not science, but track and field. From 1974 to 1981 Karl Anker Jørgensen was a member of the national team representing Denmark at international competitions, especially in decathlon and 110-meter hurdles. He won several Danish championships in decathlon, 110-meter hurdles, and for teams, and in 1975 he won the Nordic Junior Championship in decathlon. He obtained his Ph.D. in 1984 under the guidance of S.-O. Lawesson and J. Linderberg. In 1985 he did postdoctoral work with R. Hoffmann at Cornell University, where he was introduced to catalysis. The stay with Hoffmann also opened his eyes that "chemistry is more than chemistry."

Karl Anker Jørgensen was appointed as assistant professor at Århus University in 1985, as associate professor in 1988, and as professor in 1992. Since 1997 he also has been the Director of the Center for Catalysis at Århus University. In 1995 he received the Bjerrum Medal and in 2000, the Villum Kann Rasmussen Prize and the Lundbeck Foundation Nordic Research Prize. He is a member of The Royal Danish Academy of Sciences and Letters and The Danish Academy of Technical Sciences.

Scientific Sketch

The scientific work of Jørgensen includes both experimental and applied theoretical chemistry. From the beginning of the 1990s, his main interest has been the development of new catalytic asymmetric reactions. During this period the research group was also engaged in developing catalytic enantioselective hetero-*Diels-Alder* reactions (*Angew. Chem. Int. Ed.* **2000**, *39*, 3558). These reactions include the catalytic enantioselective hetero-*Diels-Alder* reaction of carbonyl compounds with both normal electron demand (*J. Am. Chem. Soc.* **1998**, *120*, 8599) and inverse electron demand (*Angew. Chem. Int. Ed.* **1998**, *37*, 2404) and the application of these reactions in total synthesis. More recently Jørgensen contributed to the development of catalytic asymmetric *Friedel-Crafts* reactions, e.g., the addition of aromatic compounds to α-imino esters catalyzed by BINAP-copper(I) complexes (Fig. 1) has shown to be an easy entry to optically active aromatic α-amino acids (*Angew. Chem. Int. Ed.* **2000**, *39*, 4114). These reactions proceed well for both aromatic and heteroaromatic compounds, and the products are obtained with high enantiomeric excess.

Figure 1. Enantioselective *Friedel-Crafts* reaction.

The *Friedel-Crafts* addition of aromatic and heteroaromatic compounds to carbonyl compounds (*J. Am. Chem. Soc.* **2000**, *122*, 12517) and alkenes (*Angew. Chem. Int. Ed.* **2001**, *40*, 160) was also developed, and for these reactions chiral bisoxazoline-copper(II) complexes were found to be the catalysts of choice.

The group has also contributed various types of catalytic enantioselective *Henry* reactions. The first contribution was the aza-*Henry* reaction of PMP-protected α-imino esters with nitronates in the presence of chiral bisoxazoline-copper(II) complexes as catalysts (Fig. **2**, *J. Am. Chem. Soc.* **2001**, *123*, 5843).

Figure 2. Enantioselective *Henry* reaction.

Based on the concept that a *Lewis* acid can initiate a keto-enol tautomerization, the first direct α-amination reaction was disclosed (Fig. **3**, *J. Am. Chem. Soc.* **2002**, *124*, 2420). This reaction provided a simple synthetic approach to syn-β-amino-α-hydroxy esters, which are highly valuable chiral fragments in many pharmaceutical products.

Figure 3. Enantioselective enolate amination.

A Crustacean Catastrophe

Starting materials (serves 6):

100 g butter

oysters

mussels

shrimp

125 mL white wine

salt

pepper

a small bunch of dill weed

a couple sprigs of thyme

Melt the butter in a saucepan with a tightly fitting lid. When the butter has melted, put all the seafood into it.

Add the white wine, salt, pepper, and the fresh herbs and cover. Let the whole wonderful mixture steam for 3–5 minutes.

The seafood can be served with a few slices of smoked salmon and lemon fruit or, its mirror-image, orange fruit in quarters.

Serve with good bread and butter and white wine.

A good Italian white wine will be excellent to accompany this dish (KAJ).

Tenderloin of Wild Boar

Starting materials (serves 6):

2 wild boar tenderloins, (1 kg each)

2 tbsp mustard

10 crushed juniper berries

a good beer

salt

melted honey

As a main course, the Vikings might have served tenderloin of wild boar with mushrooms or other fungi fried in butter, cabbage in white sauce with horseradish, and bread. After the discovery of America and the potato-German's immigration to Denmark, it would have been served with boiled potatoes.

Make a marinade from the beer, juniper, mustard, and salt and marinate the tenderloins for 1 hour. Heat the oven to 200 °C. Roast the meat for 15–20 minutes, but baste with melted honey while it roasts. Can be served with boiled potatoes.

An Italian red wine: Vino Nobile di Montepulciano is my favorite (KAJ).

The Royal M&M Almond Cake

Starting materials (serves 6):

12 stiffly whipped egg whites

350 g icing sugar

500 g finely ground almonds, unpeeled

2 baking pans lined with wax paper

100 g frozen raspberries

28 g sugar

500 mL whipping cream

1 bag of M&M's

This cake has its origin from Århus Festival Week's biggest event ever – Kosmopolitan – where it acquired its present form and name. Chili John: "The Crown Prince of Denmark, Frederik, was coming to see the Stone Temple Pilots, so we had to be hospitable – we owed him a favor. There was only almond cake and whipped cream left from the dessert, and so according to the principle of using the available garnish, that's what we used: one bag of M&M's."

Heat the oven to 175 °C. First fold the icing sugar into the stiffly whipped egg whites and then fold in the ground almonds. Put half of the mixture in each of the two equally sized pans and bake for about 35 minutes. Blend the frozen raspberries with sugar. When the cake is cold, spread this mixture onto one of the cakes and put the other one on the top of it. Whip the cream, spread it over the cake, and then decorate with the M&M's.

Port wine – Feist 1977 – is my favorite to accompany this cake (KAJ).

A Gastronomic Rock n' Roll World Tour

«My wife is an excellent cook and I have to confess that I can't cook at all – I am able to grill fish and steak – that's it!

For both my wife and me (and also our kids – I think), art plays a central part in our life. We have several friends who are professional artists, working as, e.g., painters and musicians. One of our friends writes the lyrics and music, and is the front figure in tv2 (www.tv-2.dk), one of the most popular Danish rock bands. He introduced us to Chili John (www.chilijohn.com). I am sure that Chili John's artistic cooking has not only made a whole lot of musicians – and a lot of other people for that matter – both replete and happy, but also that his food has sneaked its way into countless concerts and recordings.

Over the last 15 years, Chili John has cooked for many different bands during concerts and recordings. Van Morrison, Willie Nelson, Bryan Ferry, Toto, Elton John, Bob Dylan, Björk, Lenny Kravitz, Rage Against The Machine, Crowded House, Ray Charles, and many other international rock bands as well as Danish bands have had concerts where Chili reinforcement was called for.

The following story is from the recording of one of Elton John's CDs which took place in the PUK studios near Århus: "There were 17 persons in Elton's entourage, and I had to take into consideration that there were vegetarians, a person who was allergic to refined sugar but loved sweet things, fish eaters, etc. In reality it is not particulary difficult, but people really appreciate it if you take their eating habits seriously. The first day was chili, the second day Chinese. The third day was a gamble – Indian – all English musicians are experts – but they applauded. On the fourth day it was Cajun – Gumbo, Jambalaya. Blackened Redfish, and Crawfish produced a standing ovation. But on the fifth day I ran into trouble. I was short of time because my assistant was ill, and she usually helped me serve the meals. But Elton noticed the crisis, came into the kitchen and offered to help. Ever since, I have always called him one of my former assistants. It was actually Elton's producer, Chris Thomas, who suggested that I write a cookbook about studio food."

I have had the privilege of being served Chili John's food many times. Recently, we had him prepare dinner for my research group, and sometimes he offers to prepare special dinners in his apartment when I have guests. Here I have chosen a three-course meal from his kitchen based on Danish food traditions. The dishes and comments are from Chili John Rasmussen, *Around the World on 80 Calories or More*, Indigo Books.»

Karl Anker Jørgensen

Alan Roy Katritzky

was born in London on August 18, 1928. He started his studies at the University of Oxford, finishing up with a D. Phil. in 1954. After some years as postdoctoral fellow and college lecturer, he became lecturer at the University of Cambridge in 1958 and two years later became Director of Studies of the newly founded Churchill College. From 1963 to 1980 he was Professor of Chemistry at the University of East Anglia and was Dean of the School of Chemical Science for 11 years. He was appointed Kenan Professor at the University of Florida, where he is at present. He became Director of the Center for Heterocyclic Compounds in 1985.

During his long and extremely productive scientific career (Katritzky is author or co-author of some 1800 publications), he obtained numerous awards. He is a "Cavaliere Ufficiale" of the Order of Merit of the Italian Republic (since 1975), Fellow of the Royal Society (since 1980), Foreign Member of the Polish Academy of Sciences (since 1991), Inaugural Fellow of the International Society of Heterocyclic Chemistry (since 1995), and Fellow of the American Association for the Advancement of Science (since 2000).

His numerous awards include the RSC Award in Heterocyclic Chemistry (1982), the Golden Tiger Award of the Exxon Corp. (1990), the Senior Humboldt Award, the ACS Florida Prize (1995), the Award of the International Society of Heterocyclic Chemistry (1993), the Kametani Prize (1999), the ACS Cope Senior Scholar Award (2001), and the Gold Medal of the Partnership for Peace Foundation, Moscow (2001). He is a Doctor *honoris causa* of 10 universities in 8 countries. He has edited some 20 scientific journals and series, among those, *Advances in Heterocyclic Chemistry* since its beginning in 1963. ARKAT-USA, the Alan and Linde Katritzky not-for profit foundation for the support of research and education, particularly in second- and third-world countries, was formed in 1999 and has established ARKIVOC, a free electronic journal.

Scientific Sketch

Katritzky's group has advanced knowledge in many areas of heterocyclic chemistry, including N-oxides, heteroaromatic tautomerism, conformational analysis of heterocycles, mechanism of electrophilic and nucleophilic substitute reactions, pyrylium chemistry, and quantitative structure-property relationships (CODESSA program). Recently he has concentrated on synthetic methodology. Benzotriazole has been established as a versatile reagent for all kinds of organic transformations. The Arnd-Eistert reaction, a homologization of carboxylic acids has been improved using a benzotriazole-derivative instead of a diazomethyl ketone. This method is superior, because no unstable diazo-compound is needed (Fig. 1, *Org. Lett.* **2000**, 2, 3789).

Figure 1. Benzotriazole-mediated homologation of carboxylic acids.

Another interesting discovery is the use of benzotriazole as a leaving group in the palladium-catalyzed allylic amination (Fig. **2**):

Figure 2. Palladium-catalyzed allylic amination.

Some important advances in formation of heterocycles have been made recently in Katritzky's group, including regioselective formations of pyrrazoles using benzotriazole-substituted acetophenones (Fig **3**, *J. Org. Chem.* **2001**, 66, 6787).

Figure 3. Regioselective synthesis of pyrrazoles.

Also aminothiophenes, biologically interesting molecules, can be built up with a benzotriazole approach: starting from acrolein diethyl acetal, 1,2-disubstituted aminothiophenes can be synthesized in five steps (Fig. **4**, *J. Org. Chem.* **2001**, 66, 2850).

Figure 4. Synthesis of aminothiophenes.

This Sauerkraut Salad is easy to make and keeps fresh for several days.

Starting materials (serves 4):

500 g sauerkraut

1 tbsp vegetable oil

250 mL diced pineapple

1 apple, diced

1 onion, chopped

1 tsp syrup or sugar

Drain liquid off Sauerkraut, but first rinse, if too salty. Add oil, vinegar, sugar or syrup, apple, onion, and pineapple and mix. Garnish with finely chopped herbs to taste.

«Being always under constant pressure means that something prepared quickly can be useful!»

Alan R. Katritzky

Horst Kessler

was born in Suhl/Thuringia on April 4, 1940. He studied chemistry in Leipzig in 1958 and moved to Tübingen in August 1961 via Berlin. After finishing his diploma thesis in 1963 under the guidance of E. Müller, he earned his Ph.D. in 1966, investigating the copper-salt-catalyzed reactions of diazomethane with aromatic compounds and continued to work on his habilitation (1969) about the detection of intramolecular mobility by NMR spectroscopy. In 1971 he became full professor at the Johann Wolfgang von Goethe University in Frankfurt/Main, where he stayed until 1989. Then he moved to Munich for a chair at the Technical University. His publication list contains almost 500 contributions. Horst Kessler has received several awards, including the Otto Bayer Award (1986), the Max Bergmann Medal for peptide-chemistry (1988), the Emil Fischer Medal of the German Chemical Society (1997), the Max Planck Research Award (2001), and the Vincent Du Vignaud Award of the American Peptide Society (2002). He is a member of the Bavarian Academy of Science and the Leopoldina in Halle. Visiting professorships have brought him to the U.S., Canada, Japan, and Israel. He also is a member of the editorial boards of 18 scientific journals, including *Angewandte Chemie* (Head of the Kuratorium), *Journal of Medicinal Chemistry*, and *ChemBioChem*.

Scientific Sketch

The main research areas of Horst Kessler are rational drug design and combinatorial synthesis of inhibitors of protein-protein interaction based on 3D structures and dynamics of the target, the ligand, or their complexes. Furthermore, his group develops new NMR techniques for the elucidation of the structure and dynamics of biomolecules and their application to peptides, peptidomimetics, proteins, and their complexes. Attention is drawn also to the synthesis of peptides, sugars, and their mimetics, as well as the application of molecular dynamics in explicit monophasic and biphasic solvents.

The first determinations of many rotation and inversion barriers in small organic molecules belong to the highlights of his research (*Angew. Chem. Int. Ed.* **1970**, *9*, 219). Further investigations made it possible to determine barriers of ion-pair recombination to covalent species directly (*Angew. Chem. Int. Ed.* **1977**, *16*, 256; *Chem. Ber.* **1978**, *111*, 3200).

The Kessler group developed several NMR techniques to determine peptide and protein structures and dynamics (COLOC, *J. Magn. Reson.* **1984**, *54*, 331), first pulsed ROESY (*J. Magn. Reson.* **1986**, *70*, 106), many delayed and selective excitation techniques (*J. Magn. Reson.* **1986**, *70*, 106), the first heteronuclear 3D NMR spectra (*Angew. Chem. Int. Ed.* **1990**, *29*, 546), the MEXICO technique for the measurement of exchange rates in proteins (*J. Am. Chem. Soc.* **1993**, *115*, 11620), and new heteroediting techniques of NOEs (*J. Biomol. NMR* **1999**, *15*, 177).

The structure of many bioactive molecules was determined, cyclosporine A (Fig. 1) probably being the first 3D structure elucidated by NMR (*Helv. Chim. Acta* **1985**, *68*, 661 and 682).

The structure parameters deriving from NMR spectroscopy of proteins and peptides are used by the Molecular Dynamics (MD) group for structure calculations. In addition, new methods for the consideration of explicit solvents in MD calculations are developed and applied for stu-

Figure 1. Cyclosporine A.

dies of flexible molecules in liquid/liquid interphases (*J. Am. Chem. Soc.* **1991**, *113*, 9566 and *J. Phys. Chem.* **1994**, *98*, 23). Furthermore, simulations and conformational analyses, especially of small cyclic peptides, and docking studies for the investigation of ligand-protein and protein-membrane interactions are performed.

Kessler also focuses his interests on the development of selective and superactive RGD mimics (RGD: amino acid sequence Arg-Gly-Asp) from linear peptides to non-peptidic drug candidates via "spatial screening" and combinatorial synthesis (Fig. 2, *J. Med. Chem.* **2001**, *44*, 1938).

X = NH, CH₂

Figure 2. Aza-RGD mimetics: combinatorial approach.

Rote Grütze
Red Gritz

Starting materials:

fresh (or, if not available frozen) red currants, strawberries, raspberries, sour cherries

juice of the fruits

lemon juice

vanilla pudding mixture

vanilla sugar

custard sauce

1 egg yolk

double cream

vanilla pod

Mix the fruits with their own juice (do not use water!) and bring the mixture to boil for a short time. Use vanilla pudding mixture to thicken the juice and add one splash of lemon juice. Do not use sugar (or at least only small amounts) to sweeten; use vanilla sugar instead. Add some fresh fruits after cooling down. Be careful not to overboil the mass.

Serve with rich custard sauce, which should be rounded off with an egg yolk, real vanilla, and double cream.

«Often, when we invited some friends over, my wife prepared red fruit pudding following her own recipe. Not only the children enjoyed this meal, and she got enthusiastic compliments.

The red color alluded to the GDR background, and the fruit pudding was mentioned several times in our home guestbook.

One day an English-speaking guest wanted to know the English name for this delicious meal, and my wife answered with "red gritz" – a name which became legendary.»

Horst Kessler

Horst Kunz

was born in 1940 in Frankenhausen (Saxony) and studied chemistry at the Humboldt University, Berlin, and at the University of Mainz. He completed his Ph.D., under the supervision of L. Horner, about the synthesis of cyclic organophosphorus compounds in 1969. His habilitation, completed in 1977, dealt with ester analogues of acetyl-choline and their application in protecting group chemistry. He was appointed as associate professor for organic chemistry in 1979 and a full professor of bioorganic chemistry in 1988 at the University of Mainz. He received the Max Bergmann Medal in 1992 and the Emil Fischer Medal in 2000. In 1998, he was elected corresponding member of the "Sächsische Akademie der Wissenschaften zu Leipzig" (Saxony Academy of Science). In 2001, he delivered the Adolf Windaus Lecture and received the Adolf Windaus Medal of the Georg-August-Universität Göttingen. He is a member of the editorial boards of *Advanced Synthesis, Catalysis Organic Chemistry* and *Current Opinion in Chemical Biology*.

Horst Kunz's research focuses on stereoselective reactions and on the synthesis and development of methods in alkaloid, peptide, carbohydrate, and glycopeptide chemistry as well as in combinatorial synthesis.

The carbohydrate moieties of glycoproteins play key roles in biological selection processes. For investigations of these biological recognition phenomena, glycopeptides of an exactly specified structure are required. The allylic protecting principle was elaborated to a novel allylic anchoring in the solid-phase synthesis of peptides and glycopeptides (*Angew. Chem. Int. Ed.* 1995, *34*, 803). The efficiency of the strategy has been demonstrated, for instance, in the synthesis of glycosylated peptide T. Recently, in syntheses of partial sequences of the tandem repeat of the tumor-associated polymeric epithelial mucin MUC-1, the advantages of an allylic anchor (HYCRON), which incorporates a polar, flexible oligoethyleneglycol spacer linked to the aminomethyl polystyrene, have been demonstrated (*Angew. Chem Int. Ed.* 2001, *40*, 366).

Carbohydrates are inexpensive natural products in which numerous functional groups and stereogenic centers are combined in one molecule. By directed regio- and stereoselective formation of derivatives, they can be converted into efficient chiral auxiliaries for controlling asymmetric syntheses. For example, *Lewis* acid-catalyzed *Diels-Alder* reactions of carbohydrate-linked dienophiles furnish the corresponding cycloadducts in high diastereoselectivity.

The process has been combined with subsequent trapping reactions of the intermediates by electrophiles, resulting in the stereoselective syntheses of α-functionalized β-branched carboxylic acid derivatives. Glycosylamines offer the possibility of versatile stereoselectve applications: in the presence of *Lewis* acids, the corresponding aldimines permit high-yielding syntheses of enantiomerically pure a-amino acids by *Strecker* and *Ugi* reactions, controlled by steric and stereoelectronic effects and by the formation of complexes (Fig. I, *Angew. Chem. Int. Ed.* 2000, *40*, 1431). They can be used with equal efficiency for asymmetric syntheses of chiral homoallylamines and for asymmetric *Mannich* syntheses of β-amino acids and chiral heterocycles, for example, alkaloids.

Figure I. Stereoselective combinatorial *Ugi*-synthesis on solid phase.

Arzgebirg'sche Schusterkließ

Starting materials (serves 4):

1.5 kg potatoes

1 onion

2 eggs

2 tbsp meal

1 tsp salt

white pepper

oil or grease

Shoemaker's dumplings from the Erzgebirge[1]
Somewhere else, probably misunderstood as "potato pancakes"

Wash the potatoes, peel them, wash them again, and grate them with a fine grater[2] into a bowl. Add the grated onion. This will examine the sentimentality of the respective cook.

Whisk eggs into the mixture, add flour and salt, and stir the ingredients into the potato batter. Add pepper in accordance with your own gusto. Pungence is an individual matter, not only in the case of taste but also in the case of thoughts and judgment. But it should not be exaggerated.

Finally, heat 3–4 tbsp oil or the corresponding amount of grease in a large pan. Best are heavy griddles, enameled inside, with the form of a small tub, like the ones that were heatable pretty homogenously on a coalfire in former times (in this case use 6 tbsp oil).

Put 2–3 tbsp of the batter into the hot oil and spread it flat to "Schusterkließ," i.e., into rounded rectangles.

While enjoying the resulting image of a large spot plate fry the pancake for about 4–5 minutes until the edges get golden brown. Turn over the "Schusterkließ" and also fry them justly and wisely for another four minutes from the other side. In the same manner, the rest of the batter is processed, while adding the appropriate amount of oil or grease, respectively.

In my personal opinion, "Schusterkließ" taste best when coming directly out of the pan, and one enjoys them together with a fresh and cool beer.

Indeed, "Schusterkließ" contain all that makes you strong, all the power carbohydrates provide. Those, who like it "sieße" (sweet), strew them with sugar, although, thus, disturbing the elegance of the helical α-glycopyranosides by mixing them with β-fructofuranosides. Furthermore, they taste good with blueberry jam or apple purée.

---

[1] The Erzgebirge (Engl.: Ore Mountains) forms the border between Czechia and Germany. It is famous for its carved Christmas articles, e.g., nutcrackers.

[2] This instrument is comparable to curious intimate questions from competitive colleagues who are used to being ahead in their knowledge.

«'Schusterkließ' are boosting resources for knights during their battle at the borderline of chemical knowledge.»

Horst Kunz

Richard C. Larock

was born on November 16, 1944 in Berkeley, California, USA, and grew up in the San Francisco Bay Area. He studied chemistry at the University of California at Davis, receiving his B.S. degree in 1967 and an Outstanding Achievement Award in Chemistry from U.C. Davis. During his studies, he participated in the University of California Education Abroad Program at Georg-August-University in Göttingen, Germany. He obtained his Ph.D. in 1972, working with Nobel Laureate H. C. Brown at Purdue University, West Lafayette, USA, on the mercuration of organoboranes. After a postdoctoral stay in 1972 at Harvard University with Nobel Laureate E. J. Corey, he joined the organic faculty at Iowa State University, Ames, USA. From 1974-1978 he was assistant professor, then from 1978–1985 associate professor, and from 1985–1999 full professor. Since 1999 he has been university professor at Iowa State University. Professor Larock was a visiting professor at the University of Hawaii in 1985. His early work on new applications of organomercurials in organic synthesis earned him an Alfred P. Sloan Foundation Fellowship (1977–1979) and a DuPont Young Faculty Scholarship (1975–1976) and culminated in the publication of two books in the area: *Organomercury Compounds in Organic Synthesis* (Springer, Berlin, 1985) and *Solvomercuration/Demercuration Reactions in Organic Synthesis* (Springer, Berlin, 1986). For his subsequent work he has received the Merck Academic Development Award twice (1997 and 1998) and the Iowa Regents Faculty Excellence Award (1998). Thirty-three patents have been issued to him, and he is also the author of two editions of *Comprehensive Organic Transformations: A Guide to Functional Group Preparations* (Wiley-VCH, New York, 1999).

Scientific Sketch

The Larock research group is involved in organometallic synthesis of carbo- and heterocycles and in the synthesis of industrially useful oils, plastics, and biodegradable polymers from natural, inexpensive, and biorenewable sources. Recently he has been involved in palladium(II)-catalyzed cyclizations and oxidations and the palladium(0)-catalyzed annulation of alkenes, dienes, and alkynes. These reactions have been employed by his research group to prepare indoles, benzofurans, benzopyrans, isocoumarins, indenones, isoquinolines, α-pyrones, and aromatic hydrocarbons (Fig. 1, *Org. Lett.* **1999**, *1*, 1551; *J. Org. Chem.* **2001**, *66*, 412; *Org. Lett.* **1999**, *1*, 553; *J. Org. Chem.* **2001**, *66*, 8042).

To demonstrate the versatility of this annulation methodology, Larock applied this coupling/cyclization process to the synthesis of the isoquinoline alkaloid decumbenine B (Fig. 2), which was isolated from the tubers of *Corydalis decumbens*, used in Chinese folk herbal medicine for the treatment of paralytic stroke and rheumatic arthritis.

Larock also develops procedures for the preparation of biodegradable industrial polymers,

Figure 2. Synthesis of decumbenine B.

elastomers, and rubbers from soybean, fish, and other natural oils. The advantages of these polymers are their low cost, ready availability from renewable natural sources, and their possible biodegradability (*J. Polym. Sci. Part B: Polymer Physics* **2000**, *38*, 2721; *J. Polym. Sci. Part B: Polymer Physics* **2001**, *39*, 60). The polymeric materials are prepared through cationic copolymerization of the natural oils with divinylbenzene and styrene initiated by boron trifluoride diethyl etherate or related modified initiators. These new materials could serve as replacements for petroleum-based polymers in numerous applications.

Figure 1. Synthesis of heterocycles via palladium-catalyzed annulation.

Chili Crock Pot

Starting materials (serves 2-3):

2 cloves garlic, minced

1–2 onions, minced

425 g ground turkey

1 large can plus 1 regular can tomatoes

1 375-g can of red kidney beans, rinsed and drained

1 can beef broth

1 150-g can tomato paste

1–2 tsp cumin powder

1 tsp oregano

1 tsp sweet basil

Sauté the garlic and onions in oil. Add the meat and brown it. Add the rest of the ingredients and simmer the chili for one hour in a large kettle or cook it all day on low heat in a crock pot. Enjoy!

«I remember fondly my days long ago as an international student at the Georg-August-University of Göttingen. Above is a recipe for chili. It is easy to make and delicious on a cold winter night in Iowa or Germany! You can let it cook all day in a crock pot, while in the lab, and it is ready to eat as soon as you get home.»

Richard C. Larock

Steven Victor Ley

was born on December 10, 1945 in Stamford (Lincolnshire, UK) and studied chemistry at Loughborough University, where he obtained his Ph.D. in 1972 working with H. Heaney. He then carried out post-doctoral work in the U.S. with L. Paquette at Ohio State University and returned to the UK in 1974 to continue postdoctoral studies with Sir D. H. R. Barton at Imperial College, London. He became Lecturer at Imperial College in 1975 and was appointed professor in 1983 and Head of Department in 1989. In 1990 he was elected to the Royal Society and moved to Cambridge in 1992, where he is currently BP (1702) Professor of Organic Chemistry and Fellow of Trinity College.

His work has been recognized by many awards, including the Corday Morgan Medal and Prize (1980), the Pfizer Academic Award (1983), the Tilden Medal (1988), the Royal Society of Chemistry (RSC) Synthesis Award (1989), the Pedler Medal (1992), the Simonsen Medal (1993), the Adolf Windaus Medal of the German Chemical Society (GDCh) and Göttingen University (1994), the RSC Natural Products Award (1993), the Flintoff Medal (1995), the Paul Janssen Prize for Creativity in Organic Synthesis (1996), the Rhône-Poulenc Lectureship and Medal of the RSC (1998), and the Glaxo-Wellcome Award for Outstanding Achievement in Organic Chemistry (1999). Recently he was awarded the RSC Haworth Memorial Lectureship, Medal, and Prize, The Royal Society Davy Medal, and the GDCh August Wilhelm von Hofmann Medal together with the Pfizer Award for Innovative Science (all 2001). Recently he received the Ernest Guenther Award from the American Chemical Society (2003). He was awarded the Commander of the Order of the British Empire in 2002. Ley sits on many national and international boards. He is presently the Chairman of the Novartis Foundation Executive Committee and was President of the Royal Society of Chemistry (UK) from 2000 to 2002.

Scientific Sketch

Steven Ley's work involves the discovery and development of new synthetic methods and their application to biologically active systems. The group has published extensively about the use of iron carbonyl complexes, organoselenium chemistry, and biotransformations for the synthesis of natural products. So far more than 85 major natural products have been synthesized by his group. It is also developing new methods and strategies for oligosaccharide assembly and combinatorial chemistry.

The direct oxidation of primary alcohols with polymer-bound oxidants has been developed recently (Fig. 1). The immobilized oxidant is PS-TEMPO, which is used in catalytical amounts, and the stoichiometric oxidant is polymer-bound sodium chlorite. These reaction conditions are very mild and tolerate a variety of functional groups, e.g., carbamates, esters, acetals, and epoxides.

R = Ph-(CH$_2$)$_4$-	95%
R = BocNH(CH$_2$)$_4$-	quant.
R = THPO(CH$_2$)$_4$-	98%

Figure 1. Direct oxidation of alcohols to carboxylic acids.

Muricatetroxin C, a higly potent anti-cancer drug, has been synthesized in Ley's group using higly sophisticated synthetic methods. Key steps are a diastereoselective addition to an aldehyde and a *Sonogashira* coupling (Fig. **2**, *Angew. Chem. Int. Ed.* **2000**, *39*, 3622).

Figure 2. Retrosynthesis of Muricatetroxin C.

Recently, multicomponent reactions have been developed in Ley's group: two consecutive *Michael* additions allow the synthesis of a great variety of complex structures (Fig. **3**, *Angew. Chem. Int. Ed.* **2001**, *40*, 4763).

Figure 3. Diastereoselective consecutive *Michael*-additions.

Ley's Low-Calorie, Chemical-Free Risotto?

Ingredients to be put out on the bench:

finely chopped celery (half a wine glass)

Arborio rice (one wine glass)

white wine (one wine glass)

garlic (lots)

chunky chopped wild mushrooms (preferably freshly picked in the Black Forest whilst walking with friends)

chicken stock... hot and lots of it

torn up rocket leaves

slivers of fresh parmesan cheese

Hidden ingredients:

butter

cold-pressed extra virgin olive oil

good red wine one/two bottles - opened early so that they have time to breathe

good white wine, one bottle possibly two

Method:

Fry the mushrooms and garlic in a little olive oil. Add generous knob of butter when wife is not looking! Possibly fill her glass with wine to divert attention. Drink one glass of white wine. Set mushrooms to one side. Meanwhile, in a large risotto pan, fry the celery in a little olive oil (plus more butter) until softened and you've had a second glass of wine.

Add the rice and stir until it begins to squeak, then add a glass of white wine and turn down heat. Gradually add the stock, a wine glass at a time. It is advisable to use a different glass for this. By the time you have drunk the rest of the white wine, the rice should be al dente. If not, start on the red wine until it is. Add the mushrooms and mix well (fill wife's glass so she doesn't notice that you've added another knob of butter). Turn off the heat: stir in the rocket and parmesan (saving some pieces for garnish). Serve on hot plates. Add pepper and salt to taste and a drizzle of olive oil. Enjoy with a glass of wine if there is any left!

«No need to use a balance, NMR, or mass spectrometer... just a wine glass or two!»

Steven V. Ley

Lewis N. Mander

Lew Mander grew up in New Zealand and completed his B.Sc. and M.Sc. (Hons) degrees at the University of Auckland (1957–1961), from where he moved to Australia perform his Ph.D. on steroid synthesis and alkaloid structure determination at the University of Sydney under the supervision of C. W. Shoppee, E. Ritchie, and W. C. Taylor. After two years of postdoctoral studies with R. E. Ireland on the total synthesis of diterpenes, initially at the University of Michigan and then at the California Institute of Technology, he returned to Australia in 1966 as a lecturer in the Department of Organic Chemistry at the University of Adelaide. In 1975 he was appointed to a senior fellowship in the Research School of Chemistry (RSC) at the Australian National University, Canberra, and in 1980, to his current position as Professor of Chemistry. During the periods 1981–1986 and 1992–1995, he served as Dean of the RSC.

He has been a Nuffield Fellow at Cambridge University (1972) (with A. R. Battersby), a Fulbright Senior Scholar at the California Institute of Technology (1977) and at Harvard University (1986) (with D. A. Evans on both occasions), and an Eminent Scientist of RIKEN (1995–1996, Saitama, Japan).

In 1983 he was elected Fellow of the Australian Academy of Science and in 1990 was elected Fellow of the Royal Society. Furthermore, he is an Honorary Fellow of the Royal Society of New Zealand and a Distinguished Alumnus Professor of the University of Auckland. Among his numerous awards are the H. G. Smith and Birch Medals of the Royal Australian Chemical Institute, the David Craig Medal of the Australian Academy of Science, and the Flintoff Medal and CIBA Award in synthetic organic chemistry of the Royal Society of Chemistry.

Scientific Sketch

Mander's research interests are concerned primarily with methodology and strategies for the total synthesis of complex natural products that have interesting biological properties, such as gibberellic acid (**1**), the antheridiogen (**2**), harringtonolide (**3**), and the galbulimima alkaloid (**4**). Arising out of these endeavors has been the development of a range of useful methodologies, including *Birch* reductions, diazoketone-based chemistry, refinements to the *Wittig* reaction, unusual aldol and *Michael* reactions, and the use of cyanoformates for the kinetically controlled C-acylation of enolate anions.

1

2

3

4

Another major interest embraces the gibberellin family of plant bioregulators (*Chem. Rev.* **1992**, *92*, 573). He is concerned with the isolation (*Phytochemistry* **2002**, *59*, 679; **2000**, *55*, 887; **1996**, *43*, 23), synthesis (*Tetrahedron Lett.* **1996**, *37*, 723), structure determination, and biosynthesis of natural plant growth regulators with special reference to the gibberellins (GAs). GAs affect every aspect of plant growth and development, but their most typical (and spectacular) property is the induction of stem growth. The phenomenon of bolting in rosette plants (e.g., spinach and radish) is caused naturally by endogenous GAs (*J. Jpn. Hortic. Sci.* **1999**, *68*, 527), while the hybrid vigor obtained in maize has been shown to be due to the production of higher than normal levels of GAs. Flowering is stimulated by GAs (*Physiol. Plant.* **2001**, *112*, 429; **2000**, *109*, 97), which can also delay senescence, promote the germination of seeds, and eliminate the need for vernalization (winter chilling) in the growth of bulbs and tubers. GAs are associated with the breaking of winter dormancy and stimulate the formation of hydrolases and amylases.

One of his studies on the biology of GAs, pursued in collaboration with groups in CSIRO Plant Industry and the University of Calgary, has led to the discovery of semi-synthetic derivatives that selectively promote flowering but little or no growth (*Phytochemistry* **1998**, *49*, 1509); somewhat surprisingly, some analogues actually inhibit growth. There is a major demand for growth retardants in agriculture, and because these modified GAs can be expected to be environmentally benign, they have considerable commercial potential (*Japanese Journal of Crop Science* **1999**, *68*, 362; *Acta Horticulturae* **1995**, *394*, 199). A new project is directed towards the identification of GA molecular receptors.

Chicken Dijonnais

**Starting materials
(serves 4):**

500 g skinned chicken thighs

20 mL olive oil

20 mL brandy (optional)

100 mL white wine

2 cloves garlic

10 mL smooth Dijon
mustard

freshly ground pepper

200 mL chicken stock

few sprigs of fresh thyme or
tarragon

Pat chicken pieces dry with kitchen paper and brown in frypan with the oil.

Flambé with brandy.

Add wine, peeled and crushed garlic, mustard, pepper, stock, and thyme (tarragon).

Mix well, cover, and simmer over very low heat for 40 minutes.

Remove thyme, separate liquid, and keep chicken pieces warm.

Reduce liquid to desired consistency and pour over chicken.

Serve with a Chardonnay, Australian, of course.

«For me, cooking is too much like a busman's holiday.
Fortunately, I am married to a superb cook (also an organic
chemist). The above recipe is selected from her repertoire
and is one of my favorites.»

Lew Mander

Johann Mulzer

was born on August 5, 1944 in Prien/Chiemsee (Germany). He studied chemistry at the University of Munich, where he obtained his Ph.D. in 1974 under the guidance of Prof. R. Huisgen. After a post-doctoral year at Harvard University with E. J. Corey, he returned to the University of Munich, where he made his habilitation in 1980. After being research associate for two years at the same university, he became associate professor in 1982 at the University of Düssel-dorf. He was appointed full professor in 1984 at the Free University of Berlin, moved to the University of Frankfurt in 1995, and accepted a chair at the University of Vienna in 1996. His scientific work has been honored with the Jost Henkel Award (1982), the Leibniz Award (1994), the Ernst Schering Award (1997), and the Erwin Schrödinger Award (1999).

Scientific Sketch

The scientific work of Johann Mulzer includes the design of bidental auxiliaries (*J. Org. Chem.* **2000**, *65*, 6540) and, mainly, the synthesis of natural products. Recent examples are the total syntheses of huperzine A (*Tetrahedron Lett.* **2000**, *41*, 9229), the convergent and stereo-controlled total synthesis of laulimalid using *Sharpless* asymmetric epoxidation (Fig. I, *Angew. Chem. Int. Ed.* **2001**, *40*, 3842; *Tetrahedron Lett.* **2000**, *41*, 6323), and the synthesis of the epothilones.

Figure I. Laulimalid.

Mulzer's research group has achieved easy access to four out of five of the naturally occurring epothilones (*J. Org. Chem.* **2000**, *65*, 7456). By repeating the synthesis, but introducing the epoxide group at an early step, he has also demonstrated that the epoxide is more stable to a lot of chemical reaction conditions than most scientists thought (Fig 2, *Angew. Chem. Int. Ed.* **2000**, *39*, 581).

Furthermore, he discovered a new type of palladium-catalyzed redox reaction. Elucidation of the mechanism revealed that the reaction

epothilone A : R_1 = Me, R_2 = H
epothilone B : R_1 = Me, R_2 = Me
epothilone C : epothilone A without epoxide
epothilone D : epothilone B without epoxide
epothilone E : R_1 = CH_2OH, R_2 = H

Figure 2. Epothilones, new anti-cancer agents.

proceeds intramolecularly and forms enones from 2-(2-bromobenzyl)-ketones with an over-all loss of HBr (Fig. **3**, *Org. Lett.* **2001**, *3*, 1495).

Figure 3. Palladium-catalyzed intramolecular redox reaction.

Powidltatschkerl (Plum Dumplings)

Starting materials (serves 4):

400 g mealy apples

120 g flour

salt

30 g fine semolina

80 g butter

2 eggs

2 tbsp rum

grated lemon skin

150 g Powidl (plum mousse)

sugar

cinnamon

bread crumbs

Cook 400 g of mealy apples and press them while warm through a press. After cooling, add flour, a pinch of salt, fine semolina, 30 g of butter, 2 yolks, 2 tbsp rum, and some grated lemon peel. Knead the mixture to a dough and let it stand for 30 minutes. In the meantime, stir the Powidl (not too sweet plum mousse, preferably imported from Vienna), 2 tbsp sugar, and some cinnamon. Roll the dough onto a floured board and cut out circles of approx. 8 cm diameter. Spread egg white on the rims and 1 tsp Powidl mixture in the center. Then fold the circle to dumplings. Put the dumplings into lightly salted boiling water for approx. 7–9 minutes. In the meantime, roast 3 tbsp bread crumbs with 50 g butter in a pan. Take the dumplings out of the water, let them drop, roll them in roasted bread crumbs and dust with icing sugar. Serve slightly warm.

Vienna cuisine

«The remarkable characteristic of Vienna´s cuisine is that most of it is imported, due to the high number of Bohemian cooks and domestic helpers, who worked in the 19th century in the Danube metropolis. More than the K & K Army, the political confusion and language of the era, and the emperor Franz-Josef's relationship with Sissy, this mixed cuisine proved to be a "corporate identity" and fortification for the crumbling Danube monarchy. Like the "Wiener Schnitzel" (cutlet) and the "Wiener Gulasch" (goulash), the Vienna flour dishes, which can be a sweet or not-so-sweet main meal or even served as a dessert, come mostly only from the crown countries. Thus, the "Powidltatschkerln" (plum dumplings) have their origin not at the Danube but at the Moldau.»

Johann Mulzer

Ei-ichi Negishi

grew up in Japan and received his baccalaureate degree in 1958 from the University of Tokyo. He worked as a research chemist at the Japanese chemical company Teijin, Ltd. He came to the U.S. as a Fulbright scholar in 1960 and earned a Ph.D. in organic chemistry in 1963 from the University of Pennsylvania. Negishi resumed his post at Teijin, but returned to the United States in 1966 for postdoctoral work in organoborane chemistry in H. C. Brown's laboratories at Purdue University. After holding a series of academic positions at Purdue and Syracuse, Negishi became a chemistry professor at Purdue in 1979. In 1999 he became the inaugural H. C. Brown Distinguished Professor. Negishi's research has earned him numerous awards and honors, including the J. S. Guggenheim Memorial Foundation Fellowship (1987), the A. R. Day Award (1996), the Chemical Society of Japan Award (1997), the Organometallic Chemistry Award from the American Chemical Society and the Herbert N. McCoy Award (both given in 1998), the Alexander von Humboldt Award, Germany (1998–2001), and the Sir Edward Frankland Prize Lectureship from the Royal Society of Chemistry (2000). He has given lectures throughout the world. Beside several patents and a few dozen essays, he has published about 300 scientific papers, some of which belong to the most cited papers of synthetic organic chemists.

Scientific Sketch

In his early years, Ei-ichi Negishi began developing new organometallic reactions. One of his first chemical breakthroughs was the development of the zirconium-catalyzed carboalumination of terminal alkynes. With this method, trisubstiuted double bonds can be generated in a stereoselective fashion. (Fig. 1, *J. Am. Chem. Soc.* **1978**, *100*, 2252).

Figure 1. Zirconium-catalyzed carboalumination of terminal alkynes.

This methodology has been extended to terminal alkenes. By using a chiral zirconium complex, these double bonds can be aluminated and afterwards oxidized in an enantioselective manner (Fig. 2, *J. Am. Chem. Soc.* **1995**, *117*, 10771).

R = Hex: 88%, 72% *ee*
R = Ph : 30%, 85% *ee*
R = Bn : 77%, 70% *ee*

Figure 2. Enantioselective carboalumination of terminal alkenes.

Negishi discovered the nickel-catalyzed cross-coupling reaction of organoaluminum compounds. This was improved to one of the first palladium-catalyzed carbon-carbon bond-forming reactions, which led to the subsequent developments of the *Stille* and *Suzuki* reactions. One of Negishi's latest improvements to this cross-coupling reaction deals with coupling of electron-deficient alkynylzinc-compounds with aryl halides (Fig. 3). This is not practical with the *Sonogashira* coupling.

Figure 3. Palladium-catalyzed cross-coupling reaction of alkynylzinc compounds.

Another important field of research is the cyclization of enynes using a zirconium catalyst. This method was used to synthesize (±)-7-*epi*-β-bulnesene (Fig. 4; *J. Org. Chem.* **1997**, *62*, 1922).

Figure 4. The eneyne-cyclization reaction.

Another example of the application of transition metal catalysis is the so-called "zipper" reaction, a palladium-catalyzed cyclic cascade carbopalladation. An oligoyne is carbopalladated subsequently, and a pentacycle is formed in one reaction starting from an acyclic precursor (Fig. 5, *J. Am. Chem. Soc.* **1994**, *116*, 7923).

Figure 5. The "zipper" reaction.

Goma-ae with White Sesame, Goma-yogoshi with Black Sesame
by Sumire and Ei-ichi Negishi

Starting materials (serves 4-5):

5 tbsp sesame, well roasted and ground

1.5 tbsp soy sauce

1 pinch salt or as needed

1.5 tbsp sugar or an amount to your taste

boiled vegetable of your choice, boiled to your taste, squeeze or apply any other methods to remove an excess of water. Your vegetable items should not be soggy. Examples of commonly used vegetables include spinach, any other soft green leaf vegetables, string beans, green asparagus, etc.

Experimental procedure

1. Mix well the first four "S"-items, i.e., sesame, soy sauce, salt, and sugar.

2. Pour the product mixture onto the boiled and partially dehydrated vegetables.

You may or may not mix the whole thing. It depends. For example, you normally mix if green beans are used. On the other hand, boiled spinach is squeezed and nicely cut into ca. 3 cm long layered bunch. Just pour the sauce.

It is simple and versatile. Above all, it is healthy.

Good luck,

Ei-ichi

«According to the ancient oriental tradition, Man is reborn after a cycle of 60 years. The history of mankind has indicated that the second 60-year cycle is generally, at least somewhat, more difficult than the first. With this in mind, I wish to present a token supply of roasted white and black sesame along with one of the simplest possible recipies. Sesame has long been considered, and perhaps even is proven, to be a food item for longevity.

So regardless of whether or not you like my recipe, I recommend that you use it frequently.»

Ei-ichi Negishi

Kyriacos C. Nicolaou

was born on July 5, 1946 in Cyprus where he grew up and went to school until the age of 18. In 1964, he went to England to spend two years learning English and preparing to enter university. He studied chemistry at the University of London (B.Sc. 1969, Bedford College; Ph.D. 1972, University College, with Professors F. Sondheimer and P. J. Garratt). He moved to the United States and joined - after postdoctoral appointments at Columbia University (1972–1973, Professor T. J. Katz) and Harvard University (1973–1976, Professor E. J. Corey) - the faculty at the University of Pennsylvania, where he rose through the ranks to become the Rhodes-Thompson Professor of Chemistry. Since 1989, he has held joint appointments at the University of California, San Diego, and The Scripps Research Institute, La Jolla (Darlene Shiley Professor of Chemistry, Chairman of the Department of Chemistry). In 1996, he was additionally appointed Aline W. and L. S. Skaggs Professor of Chemical Biology in The Skaggs Institute for Chemical Biology, The Scripps Research Institute. His work is published in more than 500 papers and 50 patents, and he has supervised the training of hundreds of Ph.D. students and postdoctoral researchers. He serves on the Scientific Advisory Board of numerous scientific journals and is an advisor to several biotechnology and pharmaceutical companies. Among K. C. Nicolaou's numerous awards and honors are the Tetrahedron Prize, the Schering Prize (Germany), the Max Tishler Prize Lecture (Harvard), the Yamada Prize (Japan), the Janssen Prize (Belgium), the Nagoya Medal (Japan), the Centenary Medal (Royal Society UK), the Paul Karrer Medal (Switzerland), the Inhoffen Medal (Germany), the Nichols Medal (USA), the Linus Pauling Medal (USA), the Esselen Award (USA), the ACS Award for Creative Work in Synthetic Organic Chemistry (USA), the ACS Guenther Award in Natural Products Chemistry (USA), and several honorary degrees. He is a Fellow of the American Academy of Arts and Sciences, a member of the National Academy of Sciences, and a Foreign Member of the Academy of Athens.

Scientific Sketch

Overall, Nicolaou's programs are based on sophisticated synthetic organic chemistry and are directed towards the construction of novel molecular architectures of natural or designed origins. Emphasis is placed on both biomedical relevance and the advancement of organic synthesis as a science for its own sake.

In addition to these target-oriented programs, the discovery and development of new synthetic technologies are pursued (*Angew. Chem. Int. Ed.* **2000**, *39*, 622, 625), including new reactions (Fig. **2**) and combinatorial solid-phase synthesis for new molecular diversity, e.g., in the synthesis of epothilone and its derivatives to reveal struc-

Figure 1. Taxol™ and brevetoxin A.

During the past few years he has developed many total syntheses of bioactive natural products and their derivatives, such as Taxol™ and brevetoxin A (Fig. 1, *Nature* **1994**, *367*, 260; *Nature* **1998**, *392*, 264), oligosaccharides (*Angew. Chem. Int. Ed.* **2001**, *40*, 1576), enediyne anticancer agents (*Angew. Chem. Int. Ed.* **1993**, *32*, 1377), DNA-interacting molecules, cholesterol-lowering compounds (*Angew. Chem. Int. Ed.* **1999**, *38*, 1669), epothilones (*Angew. Chem. Int. Ed.* **1998**, *37*, 2014), antibiotics (*Angew. Chem. Int. Ed.* **1999**, *38*, 2097), and the CP molecules (*Angew. Chem. Int. Ed.* **2002**, *41*, 2678). The design of bioactive molecules is often based on a combination of molecular modeling and biological studies (*Proc. Natl. Acad. Sci. USA* **2000**, *97*, 2904).

ture-activity relationships (*Nature* **1997**, *387*, 268), and the synthesis of a large library of benzopyrans (*J. Am. Chem. Soc.* **1999**, *121*, 9939, 9954, 9968) from which several biologically active ligands have emerged. Thus a modular high-output system has been designed and developed. The system employs three technological innovations to achieve its high efficiency and reliability: (1) development of enabling technologies for solid-phase chemistry; (2) application of microreactors as the reaction units in solid-phase synthesis; and (3) use of radiofrequency tagging as the non-chemical tracking method.

Figure 2. The reaction of *Dess-Martin* periodinane and IBX with anilides and related compounds.

Fish & Chips

**Starting materials
(serves 4):**

1.3 kg Northern European
Halibut (or Cod)

all-purpose flour (preferably
special batter mix flour for
fish & chips, pale yellow)

H_2O

1.3 kg potatoes

vegetable oil

cider vinegar

salt

lemon juice

Cut filet of fish into pieces (1.5–2.5 cm thick, 4–6.5 cm wide, 15–20 cm long). Wash with H_2O, dry with paper towel, and marinate in lemon juice for 0.5 to 1 hour.

Prepare batter by mixing flour with H_2O, stirring until a homogenous, free-flowing slurry is formed (thin).

Roll fish pieces into dry flour to cover all around before dipping into batter slurry and deep-frying in hot oil until golden yellow-brown (approx. 10 minutes).

Clean potatoes, cut them into long strips, and deep-fry them in separate vegetable oil until they become golden yellow-brown chips (french fries).

Serve fish & chips with salt and vinegar (or lemon) while hot.

Enjoy with Franken or Alsatian white wine.

«This little recipe has sentimental value to me, since I learned it long before I became a synthetic organic chemist – during my struggles for survival in England as a student and a fish & chips chef.
The accompanying photos will remind you of me then and now!»

Kyriacos C. Nicolaou

Leo Armand Paquette

was born in 1934 in Worcester, Massachusetts, and received his B.S. from Holy Cross College in 1956 and his Ph.D. from MIT in 1959. In the same year, he began his career at the Upjohn Company, where he worked until 1963. From there, Paquette joined the faculty of The Ohio State University, Columbus, where he was promoted to associate professor in 1966 and full professor in 1969. He held the title of Kimberly Professor from 1981 to 1987 and was promoted to Distinguished University Professor in 1987. He has held visiting faculty positions at several universities in the United States, France, and Germany. His work has given rise to more than 1150 research publications, 38 book chapters, 17 edited book volumes, one encyclopedia, and 40 patents to his credit.

Paquette's honors include an Alfred P. Sloan Fellow, the Outstanding Young Man of America, a Morley Medal from the Cleveland ACS Section, a Guggenheim Fellow, an ACS Award for Creative Work in Synthetic Organic Chemistry, election to the National Academy of Sciences in 1984, an Arthur C. Cope Senior Scholar Award, a Senior Humboldt Award, Fellow of the Japanese Society for the Promotion of Science, the Ernest Guenther Award of the ACS, the Distinguished International Award of the National Science Council of the Republic of China, the First France/Belgium Award for Research Excellence, and a Centenary Lectureship of the Royal Chemical Society. Paquette has held memberships on various boards, including the Medicinal Chemistry Study Section of the National Institutes of Health, the executive committee of the organic division of the American Chemical Society, National Science Foundation Chemistry Advisory Committee, the Board on Chemical Sciences and Technology of the National Research Council, and the Ohio Council on Research and Economic Development, and editorial boards of ten scientific journals and annual reviews.

Scientific Sketch

Paquette's research interests include the synthesis of structurally unique natural products, the development of new synthetic pathways – particularly enantioselective and asymmetric transformations – the identification of new methods involving biochemical probes and sensors, and investigation of the use of organometallic reagents for the expedient preparation of organic compounds. His current work is aimed at the synthesis of spongistatin 1 (Fig. 1) and sanglifehrin (Fig. 2) typifies Paquette's synthetic activity.

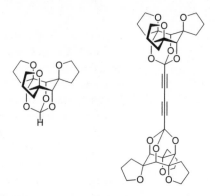

Figure 1. Spongistatin 1, a powerful toxic metabolite of red alga.

Figure 2. Sanglifehrin, an immunosupressant.

Paquette's discovery of a general approach to the construction of inositol-based, metal-ion-ligating systems has led to many exciting applications of this chemistry in bio-organic contexts. The ability of these molecules to chelate metal ions selectively is expected to satisfy the increasing demand of modern medicine for sophisticated detection methods (Fig. **3**, *Org. Lett.* **2000**, *2*, 139).

Figure 3. Inositol-based, metal-ion-liganding molecules.

Paquette's group is also concerned with defining new aspects of organometallic applications. The zirconocene-promoted enantiospecific ring contraction of carbohydrate precursors represents an example of Paquette's involvement with this complex structure chemistry (Fig. **4**, *Org. Lett.* **2002**, *4*, 1927).

Figure 4. Enantiospecific zirconocene-mediated ring contraction.

Paquette's Favorite Lasagna

Starting materials (serves 4):

500 g lasagna

700 g ground beef

1 package Swiss cheese

1 200-g package shredded cheddar cheese

1 200-g package mozzarella cheese

finely grated parmesan cheese

1 bottle (1.25 kg) Ragu sauce (traditional or meat)

Cook the lasagna. Fry the ground beef and mix in the Ragu sauce. In a large 35 x 25 cm pan, spread half of the Ragu-ground beef mixture. Cover with a layer of lasagna and top with a sprinkle of salt. Place Swiss cheese over the entire area. Layer another row of lasagna and cover with cheddar cheese. Place a third row of lasagna on top, sprinkle with parmesan and mozzarella cheese, and end with the second half of the Ragu-ground beef mixture. Bake in an oven for 30 minutes. Serve with garlic bread.

«The Paquette Research Group enjoys two social get-togethers a year. The first is in mid-summer, and the second occurs just prior to Christmas. On both occasions, a large amount and variety of food is served. Notwithstanding, the students invariably insist that my wife's lasagna be served. Its absence from the menu brings on deep disappointment. Indeed, large amounts of the lasagna are consumed on both occasions.»

Leo A. Paquette

Manfred T. Reetz

was born in 1943 in Hirschberg, Germany, and obtained a B.Sc. degree from Washington University (St. Louis) in 1965 and an M.Sc. degree in chemistry from the University of Michigan in 1967. In 1969 he received his Ph.D. degree from the University of Göttingen under the guidance of U. Schöllkopf. Following postdoctoral training under R. W. Hoffmann at the University of Marburg, he obtained his habilitation there in 1976, spent two years as associate professor at the University of Bonn, and became full professor in Marburg in 1980. In 1991 he moved to Mülheim/Ruhr and two years later became director of the Max-Planck-Institut für Kohlenforschung.

Among his numerous awards are the Jacobus van't Hoff Preis (Netherlands, 1977), the Chemistry Prize of the Academy of Sciences Göttingen (1978), the Otto-Bayer-Preis (1986), the Leibniz-Preis der Deutschen Forschungsgemeinschaft (1989), the Fluka Prize "Reagent of the Year 1997", and the Nagoya Gold Medal of Organic Chemistry (2000). Since 1997 he has been an elected member of the German Academy of Scientists Leopoldina Halle, and a member of the North-Rhine-Westphalian Academy of Sciences Düsseldorf since 2001. He has been an Honorary Professor of the Ruhr University Bochum since 1992 and has held many appointments during his scientific career. He was a member of the Executive Board of the German Chemical Society (GDCh) and its Vice-President in 1995, a member of the election commission of several German chemistry awards (August Wilhelm von Hofmann Medal, Carl Duisberg Prize, Karl-Heinz Beckurts Prize, Emil Fischer Medal, Adolf von Baeyer Medal, Alfried Krupp Prize), a member of the editorial boards of several highly reputed journals such as *Topics in Organometallic Chemistry*, *Russian Journal of Organic Chemistry*, and *Advanced Synthesis and Catalysis*, and a member of the Board of Trustees of *Angewandte Chemie*.

Scientific Sketch

The primary interest of Reetz's research is the development of chemo- and stereoselective methodologies in organic chemistry. Catalytic processes are the main focus, but the research efforts are interdisciplinary.

The first reseach area is the development of novel types of chiral ligands for asymmetric transition metal catalysis. New monophosphite-ligands are highly effective for asymmetric transformations, especially for enantioselective hydrogenations (Fig. 1, *Angew. Chem. Int. Ed.* **2000**, *39*, 3889).

Figure 1. Enantioselective reduction of itaconic acid dimethyl ester.

The second area of interest is the research on new water-soluble colloid metal oxides as catalysts for reductive aminations, for example. Transition metal salts such as $PtCl_4$ are hydrolyzed under basic conditions in the presence of a water-soluble surfactant such as Me_2RN^+ $(CH_2)_3CO_2^-$, leading to the formation of the corresponding surfactant-stabilized metal oxi-

des. These colloids show reaction rates in the reductive amination of propyl amine with benzaldehyde 5 times higher than those of commercially available catalysts (Fig. 2, *J. Am. Chem. Soc.* **1999**, *121*, 7933).

Figure 2. Synthesis and application of water-soluable PtO_2 colloids.

Another important research topic deals with the kinetic resolution of chiral compounds using enzymes: catalysts (enzymes) are improved by combinatorial and evolution-based methods. (Fig. 3, *Angew. Chem. Int. Ed.* **2001**, *40*, 3589).

R = *n*-octyl
R' = *p*-NO$_2$C$_6$H$_4$

Figure 3. Kinetic resolution of racemic esters with an enzyme.

The wild-type enzyme provides a selectivity of 1.1:1 (E = 1) in favor of the S-acid. Manipulation of the amino acids of the enzyme leads to a selectivity of 11:1 (E = 11). Directed evolution leads to a mutant enzyme with an E-value of >51.

Herb Sauce
Frankfurt Style

Starting materials (serves 4):

1 package herbs "Herb Sauce Frankfurt Style" ("Frankfurter Grüne Soße")

or:

parsley

chervil

sorrel

cress

salad burnet

borage

chives

250 mL soured milk

1 tbsp mayonnaise

1 tsp mustard

pepper

salt

sugar

lemon juice

4 hardboiled eggs

Following a procedure by Dr. med. Elisabeth Reetz
Verified by Professor Dr. Manfred T. Reetz

Wash and chop the herbs. Add soured milk, mayonnaise, and mustard. Season with pepper, salt, sugar, and lemon juice. Shell the eggs and cut them into small pieces to be added to the sauce.

To be served with freshly boiled potatoes.

«The author does not claim the privilege of having invented the procedure to prepare "Frankfurter Grüne Soße". Indeed, this is an old Hessian dish, which is said to have been known and appreciated by Johann W. Goethe, who spent his youth in Frankfurt. Whether this is true or not is a subject of discussion among the historians, as the term "Frankfurter Grüne Soße" (or "Grüne Soße") does not occur in the Goethe archives in Weimar. Anyway, being not only delicious but also very healthy, it could have contributed to Goethe's long life (the great German writer died in 1832 at the age of 82).»

Manfred Reetz

Daniel H. Rich

was born on December 12, 1942 in Fairmont, Minnesota. He
received a B.S. degree in chemistry from the University of Minnesota
in 1964 and his Ph.D. in organic chemistry from Cornell University
(Ithaca) in 1968 with Professor A. T. Blomquist. He held postdoctoral appointments at Cornell University with Nobel Laureate V. du
Vigneaud and at Stanford University with W. S. Johnson. In 1968 and
1969 he was a research chemist in the pharmaceutical division of the
Dow Chemical Company, before joining the faculty at the University
of Wisconsin-Madison in 1970. Rich was promoted to the rank of
full professor in 1981. His research has been described in more than
220 refereed publications and recognized by a long list of prestigious
awards: the 1990 Vincent du Vigneaud Award in Peptide Chemistry,
the 1992 American Chemical Society (ACS) Division of Medicinal
Chemistry Award, the 1992 Research Achievement Award of the
American Association of Pharmaceutical Scientists, the 1992 George
Herbert Hitchings Award for Innovative Methods in the Design and
Discovery of Drugs, the 1993 ACS Ralph F. Hirschmann Award in
Peptide Chemistry, a WARF University Professorship at the Univer-
sity of Wisconsin in Madison in 1994, the E. Volwiler Research
Achievement Award from the American Association of Colleges of
Pharmacy in 1995, and an Arthur C. Cope Scholar Award from the
ACS in 1999. In addition, D. Rich has been a Fellow of the American
Association for the Advancement of Science since 1986 and was an
Alexander von Humboldt Scholar in Germany in 1993. He was a
member of the Bioorganic and Natural Products study section of the
National Institutes of Health from 1981 to 1985 (Chairman for the
final two years of his term), served as Associate Editor for the *Jour-
nal of Medicinal Chemistry* from 1988 to 1992, and chaired the Division of Medicinal Chemistry for the American Chemical Society in
1992. Currently he is Associate Editor of the new ACS journal,
Organic Letters.

Scientific Sketch

Daniel H. Rich is interested in the chemistry and bio-organic chemistry of natural products derived from peptides. His goals are to understand how a molecule stabilizes binding to the receptor molecule, to characterize the catalytic mechanisms of the affected enzymes, and to devise selective inhibitors of related, therapeutically important enzymes. His synthesis of analogues of pepstatin (Fig. 1) and the characterization of their mode of binding to pepsins by various methods have provided a general strategy for designing inhibitors of this class of enzyme that has been used to develop several therapeutic agents, including inhibitors of renin, HIV protease, and, most recently, β-secretase (*J. Med. Chem.* **1986**, *29*, 2519; *J. Med. Chem.* **1983**, *26*, 904).

Figure 1. Pepstatin.

Today, the conformation of ligands bound to target proteins can be determined by X-ray and NMR methods, but what is needed are ways to identify possible lead structures based only on the knowledge of the enzyme's ligand-binding site and to select from the many potential inhibitors those that are likely to exhibit the pharmacodynamic properties needed to obtain drugs. Rich's research group is testing various approaches for designing or creating novel enzyme inhibitors. By use of computerized structure-generating programs, thousands of potential mimics of the inhibitor are grown in the active site of the enzyme. Some of these are synthesized by his students and tested to see how well they inhibit the target enzyme. This strategy is being applied to a variety of enzymes that have therapeutic potential. These include botulinum toxin metalloproteases and various aspartic proteases including b-secretase, bleomycin hydrolase, and cathepsin L. All of these inhibitors are co-crystallized with the enzyme and analyzed by X–ray chrystallography if possible. The structure-generating program is then utilized to "create" novel non-peptide inhibitor candidates, which are synthesized and assayed. The goal is to find orally active inhibitors that might serve as lead compounds for further drug discovery. Botulinum toxin metalloprotease is one of the most selective peptidases known and needs to recognize at least 35 amino acids in a protein in order to cleave the substrate sequence. There are no known natural inhibitors of these enzymes and traditional approaches employed to inhibit related enzymes fail with this one. Recently the research group of Rich obtained the first non-peptide, low-molecular-weight inhibitor of BoNT/B peptidase (Fig. **2**, *J. Am. Chem. Soc.* **2000**, *122*, 11268). They are actively trying to modify this lead using structure-based design and combinatorial chemistry in hopes of obtaining clinically useful lead structures.

Figure 2. BABIM inhibition of BoNT/B.

Ciappino – Italian-Style Seafood Stew with Tomatoes and Basil

Starting materials (serves 4):

60 mL olive oil

325 mL chopped onion

2 tbsp chopped garlic

4 tsp dried oregano

1½ tsp fennel seeds

625 mL crushed tomatoes with added purée

625 mL bottled clam juice

250 mL dry wine (e.g., Coppola Chardonnay)

650 g cans chopped clams, drained, liquid reserved; use fresh if available

450 g uncooked large shrimp, peeled, deveined

400 g can crabmeat, drained

125 mL chopped fresh basil

Cayenne pepper

In season, fresh scallops and mussels can be added.

Heat olive oil in heavy large pot over medium heat. Add onion, garlic, oregano, and fennel seeds and saute until onion is tender – about 8 minutes. Add tomatoes, clam juice, white wine, and the liquid reserved from clams. Increase heat and boil until slightly thickened, about 15 minutes.

Add clams, shrimp, and crabmeat. Reduce heat and simmer 2 minutes. Mix in fresh basil and simmer until shrimp are just opaque in center, about 2 minutes longer. Season stew to taste with cayenne, salt, and pepper.

«We often visit our daughter who lives in Anacortes, Washington, with her husband. The Pacific Northwest is a beautiful area on the coast, and Anacortes is a port city for the ferries leaving for the San Juan Islands and Victoria, Canada. The area has great seafood, and we like to take advantage of that anytime we can. This recipe is a simple but tasty way to take advantage of the ocean offerings. It is an Italian-style stew, called ciappino. We had it with a green salad, a crusty French bread, and a great Pinot Grigio.»

Daniel H. Rich

Herbert W. Roesky

was born on November 6, 1935 in Laukischken, Germany. He studied chemistry at the University of Göttingen, where he obtained his Ph.D. under the guidance of O. Glemser in 1963. After one year of postdoctoral work at DuPont in Wilmington (USA), he returned to prepare his habilitation. In 1971 he became full professor at the University of Frankfurt/Main and since 1980 he has held a chair as a full professor and Director of the Institute of Inorganic Chemistry at the University of Göttingen. He has been a visiting professor at the universities of Auburn (USA, 1984) and Kyoto (Japan, 1992), the Tokyo Institute of Technology (Japan, 1987), and also has been George & Pauline Watt Centennial Lecturer at the University of Texas in Austin (USA, 1995) and Frontier Lecturer at Texas A&M University at College Station (USA, 1995). He is a member of the Academy of Sciences at Göttingen, the New York Academy of Sciences, the Academy of Scientists Leopoldina at Halle, the Austrian Academy of Sciences at Vienna, the Indian Academy, the Russian Academy, the Academie des Sciences, Paris, and the Academia Europaea at London. He served as vice president of the GDCh during 1995. For his outstanding research, he was given honorary doctor titles at the universities of Bielefeld, Brünn, Bucharest, and Toulouse and received many awards including the Centenary Lectureship of the RSC (1985), the French Alexander von Humboldt Award (1986), the Leibniz Award of the DFG (1987), the Alfred Stock Memorial Award (1990), the Stahl Medal (1990), the Manfred & Wolfgang Flad Prize of the GDCh (1994), the Grand Prix de la Maison de la Chemie, Paris (1998), the Wilkinson Prize (1999), and the ACS Award for Creativity in Fluorine Chemistry (1999). Roesky is editor of 12 chemical journals of international relevance. He devotes his time not only to scientific research but also to popularizing chemistry and improving chemical education. He is author of two books: *Chemie en miniature* (VCH-Wiley, 1998) and *Chemical Curiosities* (VCH-Wiley, 1996), for which he received the Literature Award of the Fonds der Chemischen Industrie (1995).

Scientific Sketch

The scientific interests of Herbert W. Roesky are very broad, as reflected in his numerous publications in the fields of inorganic synthesis (organometallic fluorides, metalsiloxanes, metallacycles, metalphosphonates, aluminoxanes, main group and transition metal clusters, and coordination polymers), catalysis (zeolite analogues), material science, and chemical vapor decomposition (BN, GaN, CdSe films).

His research group studies intensely microporous materials such as zeolites, aluminophosphonates and galliumphosphates, and transition metal analogues (*Inorg. Chem.* **1998**, *37*, 6404). Apart from the traditional use as catalysts, molecular sieves, adsorbents, and ionic exchangers, new applications are being developed for use as reaction chambers of molecular dimension, as highly ordered matrices for opto-electronical nano-switches and sensors, and as molds for carbon molecular sieves.

Aluminophosphate molecular sieves are traditionally prepared by hydrothermal synthetic methods using water as solvent. Roesky developed a novel nonaqueous route (*Inorg. Chem.* **1998**, *37*, 2450). In addition, the size of the molecules and their pores can be controlled. The reaction of tert-butyl phosphonic acid with equimolar amounts of AlMe$_3$ in THF/*n*-hexane gives the hexamer [MeAlO$_3$PtBu]$_6$ **1** and the smaller tetramer [MeAlO$_3$PtBu]$_4$ **2** (Fig. 1, *Angew. Chem. Int. Ed.* **1998**, *37*, 96).

Another main part of Roesky's work deals with organometallic fluorides, containing fluorine-metal and carbon-metal bonds with the same metal atom. They show an extraordinary reactivity, and the synthetic value of this class of compounds has just been touched, e.g., in the synthesis of transition metal-main group bonds (*Chem. Rev.* **1997**, *97*, 3425; *Angew. Chem. Int. Ed.* **1998**, *37*, 843).

Recently, a stable carbene analogue of aluminum was prepared and its chemistry investigated (*J. Am. Chem. Soc.* **2001**, *123*, 9091).

Figure 1. Novel route towards aluminophosphonate molecular sieves.

164

The 1:1:1 Mix
A boosting beverage

Starting materials (serves 3):

1 can finely chopped pineapple

1 L Cognac

1 L sparkling wine

Mix the contents of a can of finely chopped pineapple with one bottle of cognac. Cool at least for one hour. Before serving, add one bottle of sparkling wine.

This quantity is supposed to be for 3 people. The effect is quite interesting... You will stay clear-minded, which leads to high-level conversations. But it could happen that the legs become heavy. Let's say the legs cannot be moved normally, they weaken. Therefore, close-by sleeping opportunities should be arranged. Prosit!

«From my student time, I recommend it for a party night.»

Herbert W. Roesky

Gyula Schneider

was born in Temesvár, Transylvania, on October 17, 1931. The family came to Szeged in Hungary in 1939. From 1950 to 1955 Schneider studied chemistry at the University of Szeged. Afterwards he was assistant under the guidance of L. von Cholnoky at the Chemical Department of the Medical School of Pécs, where he received his Ph.D in 1959. He started his habilitation at the University of Szeged and obtained it in 1966. In the year 1989 he received the D.Sc. title of the Hungarian Academy. He was visiting researcher in 1963 with E. Schmitz at the Central Institute of Organic Chemistry in Berlin-Adlershof (GDR) and in 1979 with E. Zbiral at the Department of Organic Chemistry of the University of Vienna. After the change of the political régime in Hungary in 1989, he finally received the title of a professor. In 1990 he was Alexander von Humboldt fellow and visiting professor at the Department of Organic Chemistry of the Georg-August-University, Göttingen. During the years 1994–1996 he was the head of the Department of Organic Chemistry of the University of Szeged.

In 1996 Gyula Schneider obtained the Zemplén-Géza-Award of the Hungarian Academy and a Széchenyi professor scholarship from the Ministry of Education (1999–2002). His research in the field of carotenes and steroids is documented in some 150 publications and several books.

Scientific Sketch

The major part of the scientific interests of Gyula Schneider is focused on neighboring group participations. Ester-carbonyl interactions with the intermediate formations of 1,3-dioxenium ions have been investigated in detail during the solvolysis of *cis*- and *trans*-2-*p*-tolyl-sulfonyloxymethyl-cyclohexyl acetate and benzoate (*Proc. Chem. Soc.* **1963**, 374; *J. Chem. Soc., Chem. Commun.* **1965**, 202; **1967**, 13). These processes were characterized as (AcO-6) and (BzO-6) participations (Fig. 1).

Figure 1. Neighboring group participation.

Another useful application of a neighboring group participation is the configuration determination of the four possible 16-hydroxymethyl-17-hydroxy isomers in androstane and estrane series. Their 16-*p*-tolylsulfonyloxymethyl esters undergo either cyclization, characterized by the general symbol (O–4), or fragmentation under solvolysis conditions, depending on their configuration (Fig. 2, *J. Chem. Soc., Chem. Commun.* **1968**, 1030; *Liebigs. Ann. Chem.* **1988**, 267; **1988**, 679; **1989**, 263).

i = MeOH/KOH

Figure 2. Determination of configurations.

The oxetane condensed to ring D of the sterane skeleton, or the fragments were useful synthons for the preparation of heterocyclic steroid systems (Fig. 3, *J. Chem. Soc., Chem. Commun.* **1972**, 713; *Angew. Chem. Int. Ed.* **1998**, *37*, 2469; **1999**, *38*, 200; *Eur. J. Org. Chem.* **1999**, 3013).

Figure 3. Preparation of heterocyclic steroid systems.

Tiszai halászlé
(Tisza Fisherman's Soup)

Starting materials (serves 4):

500 g small fish

1 carp and/or other large fish 1–1.2 kg

salt

1 large onion, finely chopped

1 tbsp slightly sharp paprika

1 tomato, peeled and chopped

½ cherry paprika (optional)

1 pointed sharp green pepper

Clean and gut, and wash the fish. Catch the blood and set it aside, together with the roe or milt, in a cold place. Cut off the head and tail of the carp, and cut the body into strips about 3 cm wide - if the strips are narrower, they can easily disintegrate during cooking. Lightly salt the fish, cover it, and leave it for 1–2 hours in a cold place. Put the head and tail of the carp into a saucepan with the small fish. Add the onion and the reserved blood, pour in enough cold water to just cover the fish, and simmer gently for about 1 hour until it is reduced to a pulp. Strain through a fine sieve – don't press! – and pour in about 1 L cold water; bring to the boil. Add the paprika, the tomato, the cherry paprika (if desired), the salted fish slices, and the reserved roe or milt and cover the pan and cook over low heat for 10–15 minutes until the fish is tender. It is not a good idea to stir the soup – it is better to give the saucepan a gentle shake occasionally.

The finished soup should be served in the saucepan if possible, to avoid the fish breaking up. You can add a garnish of green pepper rings.

Note: Be careful when using cherry paprika. Not everyone likes its burning sharp taste; also, if it is very sharp, the characteristic fish flavor is lost. The remedy for burning hellfire in your mouth as a result of an overdose of sharp paprika is not to drink water, but to eat a few mouthfuls of bread (the middle, not the crust!).

Hungarian Cuisine

«A fresh green patch on the map of Europe embraced by the Alps and the Carpathians this is Hungary, lying at the crossroads of migration, caravan and campaign routes, a bridge extending between the Eastern and the Western world. The occupying Magyars had the right idea when they got out of the saddle to settle here, because this is a good place to live – but they never suspected that some "transit passengers" would also like the place enough to stay for over 150 years, others for a shorter time...

One winner in all this is unquestionably the Hungarian cuisine, which has absorbed and accepted the best flavors and finest traditions of the fiery herdsman and the monks in the monastery gardens, of the Turks and the Armenians, of the Italians and the French, the Transylvanians and the neighboring peoples, of the cuisine of the old Austro-Hungarian empire – tempering and harmonizing them, adjusting them a little to its own image, but preserving them in place. This most probably explains why Transylvanian (Hungarian) cuisine ranks alongside that of France and China.

But what is Hungarian cooking like? What makes it different from the rest? What are the features which characterize it and it alone? Do any such features indeed exist?

I am reminded of our foreign friends and acquaintances who, depending on which part of the world they came from and the local eating habits, either eloquently praise the flavors and variety of Hungarian foods or disapprove of them out of concern for their health. But most agree that although it is a little difficult, and might use paprika (sometimes sharp paprika) to excess, all in all, Hungarian cooking is a heavenly and unique experience.

Hungarians like to do things with style - for themselves and even more so for their guests, using good ingredients to prepare food and drink with pleasure and enthusiasm.»

Gyula Schneider

Lawrence T. Scott

was born in 1944 in Ann Arbor, Michigan. He received his A.B.
degree in 1966 with honors in chemistry from Princeton University,
where he conducted research on bullvalene and isomeric $C_{10}H_{10}$
compounds of theoretical interest with M. Jones, Jr. In 1970, he
received his Ph.D. degree in organic chemistry from Harvard University, where he continued working in the area of highly unsaturated polycyclic hydrocarbons under the direction of R. B. Woodward. He then joined the chemistry faculty at the University of California, Los Angeles, as an assistant professor. In 1975, he moved to
the University of Nevada-Reno, where he was promoted to the rank
of full professor in 1980 and to foundation professor in 1985. He
served as department chairman from 1988 to 1991 before moving to
his present position as professor of chemistry at Boston College in
1993.

Scott's awards include senior scientist fellowships from NATO, the
Japan Society for the Promotion of Science, and the Alexander von
Humboldt Foundation. He has served on the Editorial Advisory
Board for the *Journal of Organic Chemistry* and was elected Chairman
for the Gordon Research Conference on Physical Organic Chem-
istry in 2003.

Scientific Sketch

The design, synthesis, and study of novel organic compounds constitute the primary research activities of Lawrence T. Scott and his coworkers. The target molecules are typically chosen for their capacity to exhibit unusual molecular properties and/or abnormal chemical behavior as a consequence of unusual structural features. Uncovering and defining fundamental relationships between the structures of molecules and the properties they exhibit lie at the very root of chemistry as a science and provide the ultimate motivation for Scott's research.

Corannulene, a bowl-shaped hydrocarbon, has been synthesized in Scott's lab in a novel three-step synthesis (Fig. 1, *J. Am. Chem. Soc.* **1997**, *119*, 10963).

Figure 1. Three-step synthesis of corannulene.

On the way to Buckminster fullerenes, Scott synthesized a "geodesic dome" of molecular di-

mensions, circumtrindene (Fig. **2**, *J. Am. Chem. Soc.* **2000**, *122*, 2719).

Figure 2. Synthesis of circumtrindene.

The smallest stable fullerene, C_{60}, was built up in Scott's workgroup recently (Fig. **3**, *Science* **2002**, *295*, 1500) by the first rational, chemical synthesis of this Buckminster fullerene with an overall yield in the range of 0.1 to 1%.

Figure 3. First rational synthesis of fullerene-C_{60}.

The synthesis of the fullerene precursor was performed in 12 steps starting from commercially available bromo-chloro-benzene. Using this method, only C_{60} is formed; this seems to provide evidence for an intramolecular "zip-up" reaction.

Fruitcake

Starting materials:

250 mL water

250 mL sugar

4 large eggs

500 mL dried fruit

1 tsp baking soda

1 tsp salt

250 mL brown sugar

1 tsp all spice

lemon juice

nuts

1 gallon whiskey

Sample the whiskey to check for quality. Take a large bowl. Check the whiskey again to be sure it is of the highest quality. Pour one level cup and drink. Repeat. Turn on the electric mixer; beat 1 cup butter in a large, fluffy bowl. Add 1 tsp sugar and beat again. Make sure the whiskey is still OK. Cry another tup. Turn off mixer. Break 2 legs and add to the bowl and chuck in the cup of dried fruit. Mix on the turner if the fried druit gets stuck in the beaterers, pry it loose with a drewscriver. Sample the whiskey to check for tonsisticity. Next, sift 2 cups of salt. Or something. Who cares? Check the whiskey. Now sift the lemon juice and strain your nuts. Add one table. Spoon. Of sugar or something. Whatever you can find. Grease the oven. Turn the cake tin to 350 degrees. Don't forget to beat off the turner. Throw the bowl out the window. Check the whiskey again. Go to bed.

Who the hell likes fruitcake anyway?

«This recipe is not my original creation. It was circulating on the internet, and I thought it might be appropiate for this celebration.»

Lawrence T. Scott

Victor Snieckus

was born in Lithuania in 1937 and spent his childhood in Germany during World War II. In 1959 he received a Bachelor's degree at the University of Alberta, where he was strongly influenced by R. Sandin. After graduate work at the University of California, Berkeley (M.Sc. with D. S. Noyce), and Oregon (Ph.D. with V. Boekelheide), he returned to Canada for a postdoctoral year with O. E. Edwards at the National Research Council and then joined the faculty at the University of Waterloo in 1966. He held the Monsanto/Natural Sciences and Engineering Research Council of Canada (NSERC) Industrial Research Chair in Chemical Synthesis and Biomolecule Design from 1992 to 1998. He has held visiting professorships at the Rand Afrikaans University in Johannesburg, South Africa (1991), at the University of Zurich, Switzerland (1994), at the University of Innsbruck, Austria (1995), and at the Australian National University, Canberra (2001 and 2002). Due to his relevant scientific work, he was honored with several awards, including the Alfred Bader Award in Organic Chemistry (1993), the Humboldt Research Award (1996), the Arthur C. Cope Scholar Award of the American Chemical Society (2001), the International Society for Heterocyclic Chemistry Award (2001), and the Gedimino Order of the Republic of Lithuania (2002).

Victor Snieckus was and is a member of severeal editorial boards, e.g., the *Journal of Organic Chemistry* (1984–1989) and *Progress in Heterocyclic Chemistry* (since 1988).

Scientific Sketch

A major thrust of Snieckus' group is concerned with the development of new DOM (Directed *ortho* metallation) strategies and tactics, referred to as "die neue Aromatische Chemie" (Seebach), for the regiospecific and controlled construction of polysubstituted aromatics and heteroaromatics. Snieckus' group enjoys the challenge of discovering new directed metalation groups (DMGs, Fig. 1) and of measuring their limitations with respect to established processes. Current active areas include the discovery of new DMGs, the development of new industrially convenient conditions for metallation, and the systematic investigation of the scope of combined use of DMGs to obtain specific sequences of synthetic value, including "walk-around-the-ring" procedures. In addition, synthetic utility for heterocyclic ring construction and annelation is also a continuing general aim.

Figure 1. Directed *ortho*-metalation (DOM).

DMG's : $CONR_2$, $OCONR_2$, $P(O)R_2$, SO_2NR_2, NHBoc, OMOMju

The directed remote metallation (DreM), developed in Snieckus' group (*Chem. Rev.* **1990**, *90*, 879), means capturing the anionic species in an intramolecular way. The metallating group serves also as an electrophile; interesting products, e.g., fluorenones and dibenzopyranones are easily available using this method (Fig. 2, *J. Org. Chem.* **1991**, *56*, 1683).

Figure 2. Directed remote metalation (DreM).

Another field of research is the combination of metallation and cross-coupling reactions. By choosing halide, tin, or boron electrophiles, the products can undergo palladium-catalyzed cross-coupling reactions with aryl halides (Fig. **3**, *J. Org. Chem.* **1998**, *63*, 1514).

Figure 3. Combined metalation/cross-coupling reactions.

Cold Beetroot Soup

Starting materials:

2 cooked beetroots

2 fresh cucumbers

2 hard boiled eggs

100 g sour cream

1 L sour milk or butter milk

250 mL boiled water

8 sprigs fresh dill

250 mL scallion greens

salt

potatoes

Crush egg yolks with finely chopped scallion greens and salt. Add finely chopped cucumbers, finely chopped egg whites, sour cream, and sour milk or butter milk. Peel and coarsely grate the beet, combine with the rest, add 250 mL of boiled but chilled water, and mix well.

Serve, in individual bowls sprinkled with dill, with hot potatoes.

Martin Suhm

was born 1962 in Gengenbach/Black Forest (Germany), went to school in Portugal, and studied chemistry at the University of Karlsruhe, finishing in 1985 with a diploma thesis on nuclear magnetic relaxation investigations of benzene/hexafluorobenzene interactions. After a research year with R. O. Watts at the Australian National University in Canberra (quantum Monte Carlo methods for water clusters), he joined the group of M. Quack at ETH Zürich, where he completed a Ph.D. thesis in 1990 on the far infrared spectroscopy and dynamics of hydrogen fluoride dimers. During research stays with D. Nesbitt at JILA in Boulder/Colorado (1991, 1992) and back at ETH, larger clusters of hydrogen fluoride were investigated both spectroscopically and theoretically, leading to a detailed understanding of the unusual clustering tendency of this molecule, which serves as a simple prototype for hydrogen bonding. After habilitation (1995), awarded with a Latsis University prize, an ADUC habilitation prize), and a Dozentenstipendium (Fonds der Chemischen Industrie, 1997), he was appointed full professor at the University of Göttingen in 1997.

Scientific Sketch

Whether a gardener is enchanted by the scent of a rose, whether a drug blocks a specific enzyme in the human body, whether genetic information is read from our DNA, or whether a thundercloud forms, it always has to do with specific interactions between molecules, which are mediated via hydrogen bonds and other attractive forces as well as repulsive contacts. In short, it has to do with molecular sociology. By studying simple model systems, Suhm and co-workers try to get to the bottom of such interaction mechanisms.

A particularly elementary example is the interaction between hydrogen chloride (HCl) and water. Given sufficient water molecules, they can dissociate HCl into protons and chloride ions. This leads to hydrochloric acid, e.g., in the stomach. With only one or two water molecules per HCl, the HCl stays intact. Recently, the Suhm group has succeeded in observing the vibration of an intact HCl molecule with one and two water molecules (Fig. 1, *Phys. Chem. Chem. Phys.* **2002**, *4*, 3933), whereas in the presence of many water molecules, dissociated HCl is detected.

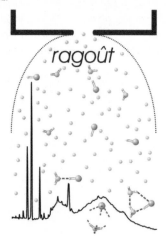

Figure 1. Schematic view of a supersonic jet expansion of HCl and water in helium and its vibrational spectrum.

For this purpose, very cold molecular aggregates are generated in a giant supersonic jet expansion, and their vibrations are probed by a Fourier transform infrared spectrometer. The technique is called ragout-jet FTIR spectroscopy (*Faraday Disc.* **2001**, *118*, 331).

In another application of this powerful technique, the ability of chiral molecules to distinguish between copies and mirror copies of themselves was investigated (Fig. **2**, *Phys. Chem. Chem. Phys.* **2002**, *4*, 2721).

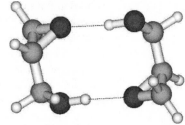

Figure 2. Glycidol dimer as one of the most elementary cases of a molecular handshake between chiral molecules.

The situation resembles that of a handshake, which feels quite different depending on whether two right hands or a right and a left hand are employed. Such molecular recognition phenomena are omnipresent in biochemistry and the Suhm group tries to characterize them in detail, using simple prototype systems where one can focus on the essential features of the interaction.

An advantage of studying small molecular aggregates is that they are accessible to high-level quantum mechanical treatments. Still, the complexity is enormous and one often has to search through maps of the interaction energy in hundreds of dimensions to find favorable structures. It is the combination of spectroscopic detection and theoretical modeling which proves to be most fruitful for the understanding of molecular sociology, the scientific study of molecular behavior in groups.

Fish Soufflé
Clausius-Clapeyron

Starting materials (serves 2):

1 small onion

40 g butter

250 g fish filets (e.g., cod or angler fish)

100 mL white wine

salt, pepper

1 bunch of dill

30 g flour

250 mL milk

grated lemon peel

4 yolks

5 egg whites

bread crumbs

Heat a small chopped onion in a pan with one half of the butter and braise the fish filets with covered lid for 10 minutes after having added the white wine. Then take the filets out of the pan, chop them, and season with salt, pepper, and plenty of dill. The liquid is concentrated (preferably in a rotary evaporator) to 1/10 of its volume. In another pan the rest of the butter is melted, the flour is added, and the mixture is braised shortly. Add the milk and the concentrated fish brew and heat to the boiling point under permanent stirring. Season with salt and pepper and some grated lemon peel and keep simmering until a thick protein-glyko-lipid mass is obtained. After cooling down to 40 °C, the yolks and the chopped fish are added. The egg whites and a pinch of salt are whipped with 5 mmol air until stiff. The fish-béchamel-mass is carefully mixed with the egg whites and filled into a greased oven-proof dish whose bottom has been covered with a thin layer of bread crumbs. The domino *Maillard* reaction is initiated at the surface by putting the dish into the preheated oven (200 °C). After 5 minutes the temperature can be reduced to 180 °C for another 40 minutes. According to *Gay-Lussac's* Law for the air and the *Clausius-Clapeyron* Equation for the steam, the bubble size increases and the soufflé gains the double or trifold volume and possibly becomes more stable. Nevertheless the soufflé should be served immediately after preparation because *Gay-Lussac's* Law and the *Clausius-Clapeyron* Equation are still valid while cooling down.

To be served with a salad.

«The soufflé should be served immediately after preparation because *Gay-Lussac's* Law and the *Clausius-Clapeyron* Equation are still valid while cooling down.»

Martin Suhm

Marcello Tiecco

received his degree in industrial chemistry at the University of Bologna in 1960. In the years 1963 and 1964, he worked under the guidance of D. H. Hay at King's College, London, supported by a NATO Research Grant. He was visiting professor at several universities in the United States. In 1972 he was promoted to a full professor of physical organic chemistry at the University of Bari. Four years later he was offered a chair at the University of Perugia as full professor of organic chemistry.

He was a member of the Scientific Committee of the Ischia Advanced School of Organic Chemistry (IASOC) from 1984 to 1994 and a member of the editorial board of the *European Journal of Organic Chemistry* and *Research on Chemical Intermediates*. In 1995 he was awarded with the Golden Medal A. Mangini from the Italian Chemical Society in the field of physical organic chemistry.

Scientific Sketch

Marcello Tiecco's field of research is the evaluation of the structure and reactivity of free organic radicals, especially the synthetic and ESR investigations, homolytic aromatic ipso substitution reactions, and cross- and homo-coupling reactions. Some of these were applied in the total synthesis of orellanine and derivatives (Fig. 1, *Tetrahedron* **1986**, *42*, 1475) and new synthetic processes promoted or catalyzed by organoselenium compounds.

Figure 1. Orellanine.

During the last few years, Tiecco and his co-workers put a lot of effort into organoselenium chemistry. They developed a multistep, one-pot procedure based on selenylation of unsaturated compounds with phenylselenyl sulfate followed by deselenylation of the addition products with ammonium persulfate. The immense advantage of this protocol lies in the fact that only catalytic amounts of diphenyl diselenide are necessary (Fig. 2, *Eur. J. Org. Chem.* **1999**, 797).
This reaction was further investigated towards the use of chiral non-racemic diselenide rea-

gents such as camphor derivatives. The conversion of β,γ-unsaturated esters or nitriles into γ-alkoxy or γ-hydroxy α,β-unsaturated esters or nitriles was performed in high yields and with moderate to good enantioselectivity (Fig. **3**, *Tetrahedron: Asymmetry* **1999**, *10*, 747).

Figure 2. Stereoselective one-pot conversion of 3-alkenols into 2,5 Dihydro-furans.

In addition to camphor ligands, the group also reported the first synthesis of a sulfur-containing chiral diselenide and asymmetric addition reactions of the corresponding electrophilic reagent to several kinds of alkenes (*Tetrahedron Lett.* **2000**, *41*, 3241).

Figure 3. Asymmetric reactions with chiral diselenide reagents.

Tagliatelle with Bologna-style Meat Sauce

Starting materials (serves 2-3):

200 g minced beef

200 g egg noodles

120 g minced pork

40 g chopped bacon (pancetta)

20 g butter

20 g olive oil

1 finely minced onion

2 tbsp chopped carrot

2 tbsp finely sliced celery

250 mL tomato purée

250 mL meat broth

½ glass red wine

salt

freshly ground black pepper

tagliatelle (noodles)

Course: pasta
Typical ingredient: ragout
Cooking method: boiling, sautéing, simmering

1. Melt the butter in oil together with the bacon.
2. Sauté the vegetables; when they are golden brown, add the meat; mixing well.
3. Pour in the wine and let it evaporate.
4. Add the tomato purée and the broth, season with salt and pepper, and allow to cook for at least one hour on low heat. If the sauce should get too thick, add some hot broth.
5. Boil the noodles in abundant salt water, drain, and dress with Bologna-style Meat Sauce

It is advisable to accompany this dish with some good red wine, such as those coming from central Italy, i.e., Rosso di Montefalco, Sacrantino di Montefalco, Rubesco Lungarotti, Nobile di Monte-pulciano, Brunello di Montalcino (very expensive) or, of course, Chianti.

Lutz Friedjan Tietze

was born on March 14, 1942 in Berlin and studied chemistry and economics in Kiel and Freiburg. In 1966 he obtained his diploma and in 1968, his Ph.D., working on the specific oxidation of laudanosoline derivatives, both under the guidance of B. Franck at the University of Kiel. After two years as a research associate in the group of G. Büchi at the Massachusetts Institute of Technology, he became scientific assistant at the University of Münster/Westphalia. After a second stay abroad with A. R. Battersby at the University of Cambridge (UK) he finished his habilitation in 1975 on the biogenesis and synthesis of secologanine. In 1977 he was appointed associate professor at the University of Dortmund, from where he moved to the University of Göttingen one year later to become full professor and Director of the Institute of Organic Chemistry. He was visiting professor at the University of Wisconsin, Madison (1982), at the EHICS Strasbourg (1995), at the University of New South Wales, Sydney, Australia (1999), and at the University of Bologna, Italy (2001). For his book *Reactions and Syntheses in the Organic Chemistry Laboratory* (German: Thieme, English: University Science Books), which he published together with Th. Eicher and which was translated into English, Japanese, Russian, and Korean, the two authors were awarded the Literature Prize of the Fonds der Chemischen Industrie (1982). Tietze is a member of the Academy of Sciences in Göttingen, a Fellow of the Royal Society of Chemistry, honorary fellow of the Society of Argentinian Chemists (SAIQO), fellow of the Japanese Society for the Promotion of Science, and chairman of the steering committee of the German Chemical Societies. In 1994 a Doctor *honoris causa* was granted to him by the University of Szeged (Hungary), and in 2002 he received the Grignard-Wittig Award of the Société Française de Chimie and the Silver Medal of the University of Szeged, Hungary. Tietze is author of some 320 publications and 22 patents.

Scientific Sketch

The scientific interests of Professor Tietze are very broad. Apart from "classical" total synthesis of biologically potent natural products such as the macrolide antibiotic 5,6-dihydrocineromycin B (*Angew. Chem. Int. Ed.* **2001**, *40*, 901) and cephalotaxine (*J. Am. Chem. Soc.* **1999**, *121*, 10264), the development of new efficient and selective synthetic methods in organic chemistry matches his focus.

His protocol for the allylation of ketones to obtain the corresponding homoallylic tertiary alcohols using norpseudoephedrine (NPE) derivative as an auxiliary is the only known method to differentiate between a methyl- and an ethyl-group (Fig. 1).

Figure 1. Allylation of ketones using a nor-pseudoephedrine derivative as an auxiliary.

Furthermore, his name is associated with the development of domino processes such as the domino *Knoevenagel* hetero *Diels-Alder* reaction sequence that was employed in the total syn-

thesis of hirsutine (1) (Fig. 2, *Angew. Chem. Int. Ed.* **1999**, *38*, 2045).

In addition to combinatorial chemistry and the application of high pressure in organic synthesis to increase, for example, the selectivity of *Diels-Alder* reactions, he is interested in the development of new anticancer agents for selective tumor therapy that are tested in interdisciplinary cooperations. Tietze has developed some highly potent prodrugs of the antibiotic CC-1065, which show excellent selectivity factors of more than 3000 between prodrug and corresponding toxin. The prodrug will be transformed into the active anticancer drug selectively at the cancer cell in the organism through glycolysis followed by a *Winstein*-cyclization, as shown in Fig. 3, using a conjugate of glycohydrolase and an monoclonal antibody, which binds to the cancer cells (*Angew. Chem. Int Ed.* **2002**, *41*, 765).

Figure 3. The highly potent anticancer agent CBI-Q and its activation due to the ADEPT concept.

Figure 2. The domino *Knoevenagel* hetero *Diels-Alder* reaction sequence used in the total synthesis of enantiopure hirsutine (1).

Pork Roulades with Cheese

Starting materials (serves 4):

4 pork roulades

1 tbsp mustard

salt

pepper

2 tbsp butter

4 slices chester cheese

1 glass white wine

parsley

The cleaned and dried meat slices are plated, salted, peppered, and coated with mustard. Then they are covered with a slice of chester cheese and some parsley, rolled up, and secured with string. Heat the butter in a pan and brown the roulades well all over. Add a little hot water and the white wine and braise the roulades, turning them occasionally for 60 to 80 minutes.

Serve them together with curry rice and salad.

The Perfect Sauce

«Andrea was standing in the kitchen preparing a delicous sauce for the favorite dish of her father. A lot of different ingredients piled up in front of her: milk, cream, salt, pepper, and a big bag of flour. Andrea was still a child and had no experience in cooking, but this sauce had to be perfect according to her ambition, because it was her father's birthday.

Andrea ladled the broth carefully out of the roasting tin with the meat rolls, put it into a small pot, and took the bag with the flour. She stirred one tablespoon of the flour into a cup and waited until the broth was boiling. Then she added the flour into the pot and stirred eagerly with all her might, preventing the formation of small lumps, because her father hated these lumps like poison. Now she had to season the sauce. But this was more complicated than she had expected. In spite of all her efforts, the sauce did not taste right. Despairingly, she tried some paprika – without success. Then she tried cream, pepper, and flavor enhancer without any success. She seasoned and tasted and suddenly the door was opened. The great master himself entered the kitchen and at first sight he checked the situation. He opened the drawer with the kitchen utensiles and took out a big spoon. Then he tasted the sauce and said: "The sauce cries for acid, don't you hear that? Two spoons of lemon juice will help in this case." And now he spoke the unforgotten and important words: "Andrea, you have to put yourself into the inside of things. Cooking is like chemistry. A chemist has to put himself into the position of the molecules. Then he knows what such a molecule wants and how it reacts. Now he is able to understand the reaction. You have to do so in the kitchen, then you can be sure that everything succeeds."»

Karin Tietze

Claudio Trombini

was born in 1949 in Ravenna, Italy. He studied chemistry at the University of Bologna, where he received his degree in chemistry *cum laude* in 1973 under the supervision of A. G. Giumanini, working on the Stevens and Sommelet rearrangements of quarternary ammonium ions. He spent 18 months as an EURATOM fellow with S. Facchetti at the EURATOM Joint Research Center of Ispra (Italy), where he was involved in the synthesis and mass spectrometric analysis of organomercury compounds. Then he joined the A. Umani-Ronchi group and worked at the University of Bologna as an Italian C.N.R. fellow from 1975 to 1979, carrying out research activities in the field of organic synthesis. His main interest focused on the development of new reduction protocols using the lamellar compound potassium-graphite, on the preparation of highly dispersed metals on graphite, and on their use as heterogenous catalysts or reagents in organic synthesis. He became lecturer (1979) and associate professor (1985) at the Faculty of Chemistry, then full professor (1994) at the Faculty of Environmental Science of the University of Bologna.

Scientific Sketch

The current research interests of Claudio Trombini include organic synthesis and environmental chemistry. The first topic is centered around organometallic chemistry directed towards the development of new synthetic methodologies; it includes the synthesis of bioactive molecules such as enzymatic (glycosidases) inhibitors (Fig. 1) starting from nitrones and the development of new stereocontrolled allylation and heteroallylation reactions based on organoboron, indium, and zinc chemistry.

Figure 1. The approach to pyrrolidine azasugars of general structure 1.

For the synthesis of biofunctional azasugars, he starts from a cyclic nitrone easily accessible from L-tartaric acid. The key reaction is the addition of vinylmagnesium chloride to nitrone 3, affording the corresponding hydroxy pyrrolidines 4a and 4b in very good yields and in a diastereomeric ratio of 93:7 independently of the reaction temperature used (Fig. 2, *J. Org. Chem.* **2001**, *66*, 1264; *Synthesis* **2000**, 759).

Figure 2. Diastereoselective key step in the synthesis of 1.

Trombini has developed new synthetic protocols that are useful for the synthesis of variously substituted homoallylic alcohols. The hydroboration of propargyl halides was at the basis of one-pot, three-component processes that allow us to synthesize (Z)-1-bromoalk-1-en-4-ols 5 or anti-homoallylic alcohols 6 (Fig. 3, *J. Org. Chem.* **2000**, *65*, 8767; *Synlett* **2001**, 601). By a suitable choice of the experimental conditions, it is possible to trap the intermediate allylic boranes with aldehydes and to steer the process towards the synthesis of either 5 or 6.

Figure 3. Hydroboration of propargyl bromide in a simple one-pot, three-component reaction.

Furthermore, he proposed the use of 3-bromopropenyl esters 7 as starting materials in new routes to 1-alken-3,4-diols 8 based on *Grignard* or *Barbier* reactions of 7 with In or Zn, either in THF or in water (Fig. 4, *Org. Lett.* **2001**, *3*, 2981; *Chem. Comm.* **2001**, 2310).

Figure 4. A new synthon for the α-hydroxyallylation of aldehydes.

The second topic is centered around the development of new analytical methodologies useful for the study of the biogeochemical cycle of mercury and of the environmental fate of persistent organic pollutants. Thus, he performed an active biomonitoring experiment using mussels *(Mytilus galloprovincialis)* as mercury bioaccumulators to evaluate mercury bioavailability in a mercury-polluted coastal wetland near Ravenna, Italy (*Environ. Toxicol. Chem.* **1999**, *18*, 1801). Epicuticular waxes of *Laurus nobilis* leaves, being the outermost surface layer of the leaf, are the primary target of air pollutants. Trombini and coworkers use this plant as a passive sampler of polycyclic aromatic hydrocarbons in ambient air (*Fresenius Environ. Bull.* **2001**, *10*, 26).

Lasagne Verdi

Starting materials (serves 10):

Sauce (ragù):

50 g butter

1 sliced onion

2 carrots

2 stalks celery

200 g minced bacon

500 g minced loin

2 glasses tomato sauce

½ glass white wine

salt, pepper

Béchamel sauce :

50 g butter

50 g flour

½ L milk

salt

Pasta

800 g flour

6 eggs

300 g spinach

½ kg parmigiano cheese

The preparation of Lasagne Verdi (Green Lasagna, Bologna style) is not so simple and will be discussed in terms of a convergent plan, familiar to chemists involved in the synthesis of complex organic molecules.

Intermediate #1: the sauce (ragù)

Fry slightly 1 sliced onion, 2 carrots, and 2 stalks of celery, both chopped, in 50 g of butter, then add 200 g of minced bacon and 500 g of minced pork loin. Leave to fry for a few minutes, then add 2 glasses of tomato sauce, salt and pepper, and ½ glass of white wine. Cook the sauce for 3 hours on a low flame with periodical mixing.

Intermediate #2: the béchamel sauce

Melt 50 g of butter in a pan, add 50 g flour, and let cook for a few minutes under continous stirring. Add ½ L of boiling milk and a pinch of salt and leave to cook for 10 more minutes, always stirring to avoid lumps.

Intermediate #3: the pasta

Mix into dough 800 g of flour, 6 eggs, and 300 g of spinach (previously boiled and sieved). Roll out a thin sheet of pastry with a wooden rolling pin (matterello, the most common tool in a Bolognese kitchen, 80 cm long × 5–6 cm diameter, sometimes improperly used in family discussions on the husband's head) in a wooden trencher (wooden tools are essential to confer surface roughness to pasta, which allows a better adhesion of sauce). Cut many 10 cm wide long rectangles, boil them in abundant salty water for 5–6 minutes, pour in cold water for 2 minutes, and spread all rectangles on dishcloths to drain them.

The final synthetic step

(Besides the intermediates #1–3, ½ kg of parmigiano cheese is needed.)
In a bake-and-serve dish (internal area 800 cm^2 for these doses), arrange a layer of sauce and sprinkle it with freshly grated parmigiano, a layer of pasta, a layer of béchamel sauce with parmigiano, a layer of pasta, a layer of sauce with parmigiano, and so on, until all the ingredients have been used up (Fig. **5**). Coat the top layer with bechamel, a few pats of butter, and some tomato sauce. Bake in a medium hot oven (approx. 150–160 °C) for about 1 hour, and finally, enjoy it!

«As often happens to us, our preferred dishes are related to our childhood. I retain a clear memory of the late 1950s when my grandmother ran a little inn in summertime at the seaside (Ravenna). She used to prepare lasagna and other kinds of pasta every day. I surely ate an industrial amount of it at that time. But I'm attracted to lasagna for a second reason related to its layered structure (Fig. 5), which reminds me of my youth as a chemist during the 1970s and 1980s when for a decade I devoted my efforts to the study of a lamellar compound of graphite: potassium-graphite.

Coming to the structure of lasagna, a vertical section is shown in Fig. 5.»

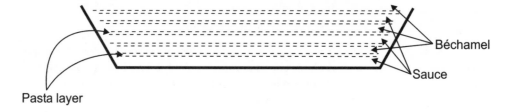

Figure 5. Scheme of a lasagna.

Essential information about Bologna

«The symbol. The two towers are among the city's most famous landmarks. In the 12th and 13th centuries, the noble families of Bologna raised more than 100 towers across the city in successive attempts to outdo each other. Of the 20 medieval skyscrapers that have survived until today, the Asinelli and the Garisenda towers are the most famous. Standing at the end of Via Rizzoli, they lean precariously in such a fashion that stereochemists consider them an example of a left-handed helix. The taller of the two, Torre degli Asinelli (98 m), can be climbed (498 steps), offering spectacular views out to the city. Its stumpy companion, Torre Garisenda (48 m), was cut down to its current size during the 14th century when its top threatened to topple it. The tradition. According to the tradition, Bologna, among Italian towns, was called la dotta (the erudite one), la grassa (the fat one), and la rossa (the red one). The last adjective is related to the dominant color of the fronts and roofs of its buildings, but after the second World War it was also related to the municipality, ruled for more than 50 years by left-wing parties.
Bologna is called la dotta because of its university (Alma Mater, with more than 90,000 students) being the oldest university in the western world. In 1988 the ninth centenary was celebrated, and on that occasion the Magna Charta of the European Universities was signed by more than 80 rectors of European universities. The aim of this document was to express the deepest values of university traditions and to encourage strong bonds among the participating European universities.
Although traditions vary and early documents are unreliable, 1088 is accepted as a conventional date to indicate when teaching became free and independent of ecclesiastic schools in Bologna. It is towards the turn of the 11th century, in fact, that masters of grammar, rhetoric, and logic began to study law in Bologna. The first scholar traditionally mentioned is Pepo, who gathered and made comments on the texts of Roman Law. There is, however, little reliable historical knowledge about Pepo; what is known about Irnerius or Wernerius is better documented. His classification of Roman legal documents was not confined to Bologna but extended to a very wide area of central and northern Italy. Irnerius' methods mark a turning point in the history of law studies, although it has not yet been ascertained whether he was the real author of those works that were attributed to him in the past. Among those are the *Quaestiones de iuris subtilitatibus* and the *Summa Codicis*. Two centuries later, Odofredus stated that Irnerius, while "studying for him-

self," was the first to pass on his research through his teaching. Irnerius was a master of the glossa, or commentary. Although he was not the first person to write glossae, undoubtedly those who followed his lessons freely made notes of the great master's interpretations in the margins of the ancient texts. With Irnerius we find the establishment of law as an autonomous discipline to be studied with precise methods. The rest of the story is available on the Web site:

http://www.unibo.it/avl /english/story/story.htm.

Finally, Bologna is called la grassa because it can be considered Italy's gastronomical capital and a city fabled for pigging out. Everybody has heard of spaghetti alla bolognese, but do not expect to find this dish here. The Bolognese call their meat sauce ragù, and prefer to eat it with tagliatelle. This pasta was inspired, according to the tradition, by the long, blond hair of Lucrezia Borgia on the occasion of her wedding ceremony with Alfonso d' Este, Duke of Ferrara. Bologna is also famous for its mortadella (baloney) - a huge sausage, often more than a foot wide, named after the mortar in which butchers used to pound the pork. But the most famous ingredient to come out of the city is the egg-rich pasta used to create tortellini. Tortellini, tiny round stuffed pasta, were modeled, according to the tale "la Secchia rapita" of Tassoni, on the form of the navel of Venus. They can be found in restaurants all over the city, typically stewed in beef and chicken broth.»

Claudio Trombini

196

Rocco Ungaro

was born in the South of Italy (Potenza province) and studied chemistry at the University of Parma, where he graduated in 1968 in the laboratory of G. Casnati. After a short stay in the pharmaceutical industry, he returned in 1970 to Parma University as a lecturer, becoming associate professor in organic chemistry in 1982 and full professor in 1986. In 1974 and 1975 Ungaro was postdoctoral fellow at the State University of New York (SUNY) in Syracuse in the laboratory of J. Smid.

He is co-author of more than 170 papers in international journals and books, including 10 review articles. He has been invited to lecture at several national and international meetings devoted to macrocyclic, supramolecular, organic, and inorganic chemistry and at several research institutions.

Ungaro has served as national representative for Italy in the European COST Actions D7 (Molecular Recognition Chemistry) and D13 (New Molecules for Human Health Care) and as treasurer of the Organic Chemistry Division of the Italian Chemical Society and is currently on several advisory committees and on the editorial board of three international journals devoted to supramolecular chemistry. In 2002 Ungaro was awarded the Research Price of the Italian Chemical Society (Division of Organic Chemistry) for "Organic Structures and Molecular Interactions".

Scientific Sketch

With his scientific work, Rocco Ungaro pioneered the chemistry of calixarenes and their application in supramolecular chemistry. In 1979, he isolated the intracavity inclusion complex of p-tert-butylcalix[4]arene and toluene, which represents the first example of a neutral organic guest, held inside the cavity of a neutral synthetic host by noncovalent interactions. He exploited the conformational properties of calixarenes to design and synthesize novel and very selective ionophores for spherical cations (Fig. 1 and 2, J. Org. Chem. **1997**, 62, 6236). He was able to show that calix[4]arene derivatives in the cone conformation are selective for sodium, calcium, and lanthanide ions, whereas those in the partial cone or 1,3- alternate

Figure 1. p-(tert-Butyl)calixa[a]arene and p-(Benzyloxy)-calix[8]arene.

Figure 2. Synthesis of p-(Benzyloxy)calix[8]arene.

conformation bind preferentially to potassium and cesium ions and conformationally mobile calix[8]arene derivatives are selective for strontium (Fig. 3, J. Am. Chem. Soc. **2001**, 123, 12182). The calixarenes can easily be functionalized to change their binding properties. If special peptides are used as substituents, calix-[4]arenes can be used as vancomycin mimetics (J. Org. Chem. **2000**, 65, 5026).

Ungaro's studies led to interesting applications in ion sensors and in radioactive waste treatment and allowed the disclosure of the role of weak intermolecular interactions (CH-π, cation-π, and π-π) in molecular recognition.

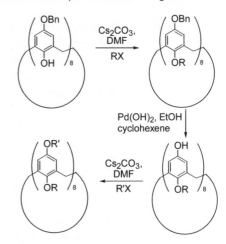

Figure 3. Derivatization of p-(Benzyloxy)-calix[8]arene.

He has also carried out important studies in the field of bioorganic chemistry, synthesizing enzyme models and novel receptors for anions, carbohydrates, and small peptides, some showing biological activity.

Pasta al Forno
Southern Italy Style

Starting materials (serves 6):

500 g penne rigate pasta (durum wheat semolina)[1]

300 g peeled tomatoes, purée (or passato di pomodoro)

300 g lean beef, ground

1 egg

1 clove of garlic, minced

1 tsp fresh parsley, minced[2]

1 small shallot (or green onion)

300 g scamorza cheese[3]

100 g parmigiano-reggiano cheese, freshly grated

60 mL extra virgin olive oil

60 mL dry white wine

salt and pepper to taste

Procedure:

1) In a bowl stir the egg and the minced garlic and parsley, add the ground meat, salt, and pepper, and amalgamate all the ingredients until a homogeneous mixture is obtained. Prepare small meatballs of ca. 1-cm diameter and set them aside.[4]

2) In a wide pan heat 60 mL of extra virgin olive oil, add the meatballs and allow them to brown evenly, then add 60 mL of white wine and continue the gentle heating. When the volume of the wine is reduced by half, add the tomato purée, the whole (peeled) shallot, some salt and stir. Reduce heating, cover the pan, and cook the sauce with the meatballs for about 45 minutes, stirring from time to time and adding water when the sauce becomes too thick. At the end, remove the whole shallot from the sauce and put it aside.

3) When the tomato sauce is almost completed, bring a pot of approx. 5 L water to the boil, add salt and boil the pasta. Drain it when it is fairly al dente (approx. 2 minutes before the recommended cooking time) and put it into a large mixing bowl. Toss the pasta with the prepared tomato sauce and meatballs, sprinkle with parmigiano-reggiano cheese (approx. 60 g), and mix well.

4) Preheat oven (180 °C), then butter (or oil) a 20–30 cm baking dish and layer it with half of the pasta. Cover it with thin slices of the scamorza cheese and add the remaining pasta to form a second layer. Sprinkle evenly with the remaining parmigiano-reggiano cheese and bake it (at 180 °C) until a golden crust (gratin) is formed on top (approx. 20 minutes). Serve immediately.[5, 6]

---

[1] Mezze penne or ziti can be used as well.

[2] Do not use dried parsley.

[3] Mozzarella cheese can be used as well.

[4] This is the "rate determining" step of the entire process: it takes approx. 45 min for one person to prepare the small meatballs. Help in this step will reduce the overall time

[5] All steps 1–4 , except baking for the last 20 minutes, can be done the day before.

[6] The pasta al forno can be enjoyed also one or two days after cooking. In this case it is advisable to warm.

«The main reason that I selected this recipe is that I grew up with it. Several pleasant events in the small village where I was born in Basilicata (or Lucania) were celebrated with a dinner having Pasta al Forno as the main dish. The recipe probably originated from Sicily and later on spread all over Southern Italy, with some small variation from region to region. The proposed one is more typical for the mountain villages of Basilicata, Calabria, Campania, and Abruzzo.

The flavors of Southern Italy were very much appreciated by the Emperor Frederick II Hohenstaufen (1194–1250), who was also King of Sicily and Germany. This recipe needs the patience of a chemist, especially in the preparation of the small meatballs, in order to be carried out successfully. Finally, the recipe is based on a wealth of successful experimental data and can be easily reproduced. Moreover, it is quite rich in calories and can conveniently constitute a complete meal.»

Rocco Ungaro

Edwin Vedejs

was born on January 31, 1941 in Riga, Latvia. He went to the University of Michigan to finish his B.S. in 1962. After his Ph.D. under the guidance of H. Muxfeldt at the University of Wisconsin, Madison, USA, in 1966, he became Postdoctoral Fellow in the group of E. J. Corey at Harvard University. In 1967 he entered the faculty of the University of Wisconsin again to become assistant and later full professor. Accepting the chair as Moses Gomberg Professor of Chemistry he moved to the University of Michigan, Ann Arbor, USA, in 1999. His research interests include synthesis, natural products chemistry, heteroelement chemistry, asymmetric synthesis, and mechanistic chemistry.

Apart from a number of grants, Vedejs has received numerous awards, among those, the Alexander von Humboldt Senior Scientist Award (1984), the Pharmacia & Upjohn Teaching Award (1996), and the Paul Walden Medal of the Riga Technical University (1997). Over the years he has been a member of the editorial or advisory boards of a number of scientific journals and series, among those, *Journal of the American Chemical Society, Journal of Organic Chemistry, Organic Syntheses, Chemistry of Heterocyclic Compounds*. He is Chair Elect of the ACS Organic Division for the years 2002–2004.

Scientific Sketch

Edwin Vedejs' work is designed to develop an understanding of conceptual, stereochemical, mechanistic, and preparative aspects of organic synthesis. Targets for total synthesis can be natural products derived from nitrogen-containing heterocycles, but they can also be complex unnatural heteroelement (boron, nitrogen, phosphorus, etc.) containing molecules that have been designed to serve as catalysts for enantioselective reactions. He uses total synthesis as a challenging testing ground for the fundamental issues that are under study in his group, e.g., the kinetic resolution of allylic alcohols with a chiral phosphine catalyst (Fig. 1, *Org. Lett.* **2001**, *3*, 535). This methodology allows us to synthesize enantiopure allylic alcohols by selective acylation of one enantiomer.

Figure 1. Kinetic resolution of allylic alcohols using a phosphine catalyst.

Recently, some analogues of the higly cytotoxic diazonamide A have been synthesized in Vedejs' group using efficient synthetic methods. The key steps are a *Suzuki*-cross-coupling followed by a *Dieckmann*-type cyclization (Fig. **2**, *Org. Lett.* **2001**, *3*, 2551). During the past year, the structure of diazonamide was revised, resulting in replacement of the acetal by an aminal (nitrogen in place of one oxygen). The synthesis of the aminal series is under study.

Figure 2. Synthesis of the macrolide core of diazonamide A.

Coupling the aryl triflate derived from indole with a boronic acid yields the two atropisomers in a 65% yield. By treating the atropisomeric mixture with LDA, the macrocylic ketone is formed in a 57% yield.

A totally different field of research is crystallization-induced asymmetric transformation: stereogenic heteroelements can be generated in good diastereomeric ratios: the principal requirement is that interconversion (epimerization) of diastereomers must take place faster than crystallization.

Pat Anderson-Vedejs' Wisconsin Linzer Cake

Starting materials (serves 4):

250 mL unblanched almonds

375 mL sifted flour

1/2 tsp cinnamon

1/8 tsp cloves

1/4 tsp salt

170 mL butter

2 egg yolks, beaten

1 tsp grated lemon rind

250 mL raspberry jam

icing sugar

Chop almonds through medium blade of food chopper to make a coarse powder. Sift together flour, spices, and salt. Blend butter and sugar until creamy; then add egg yolk, chopped almonds, and lemon rind and beat until fluffy. Stir in dry ingredients. Knead until very well mixed. Press 3/4 of dough against sides and bottom of an 20-cm pie pan and cover with a layer of jam. Form remaining dough into eight 20-cm strips 1.3 cm thick. Make a lattice over jam with four strips criss-crossed in each direction. Bake at 180 °C (moderate heat) in oven 20–30 minutes. Cool, cut into about 24 wedges, and sprinkle lightly with powdered sugar.

«The recipe that I would like to submit for your "inspection" is actually my wife's recipe for what is no doubt based on a European (Austrian?) original. My wife remembered serving this to Prof. Tietze and his wife during our months in Göttingen back in 1984, so I thought this would be the best connection that a non-cooking chemist like myself can manage (you don't want to test my recipes). Since this is all in American weights and measures, it may be an interesting challenge for you to find the conversions, as well as a linguistic test. Perhaps after all the conversions, the product will not be quite identical to that original European version. Who knows how many translations were already involved.»

Edwin Vedejs

K. Peter C. Vollhardt

was born on March 7, 1946 in Madrid, Spain. He grew up there and in Buenos Aires, Argentina, where he went to primary school. He then moved to Germany and completed his secondary school education in Munich, where he obtained a Vordiplom in chemistry at the University of Munich. In 1968 he moved to University College, London, to graduate in 1973 as a Ph.D. in chemistry with P. J. Garratt. After two years as a postdoctoral fellow with R. G. Bergman at the California Institute of Technology in Pasadena, he was appointed assistant professor at the University of California, Berkeley. In 1975 he became Principal Investigator of the Materials and Chemical Sciences Division, Lawrence Berkeley Laboratory. In 1978 he was promoted to associate professor and in 1982, to full professor. From 1983 to 1987 he was also a Principal Investigator at the Center for Advanced Materials, Lawrence Berkeley Laboratory. Since 1996 he has been Assistant Dean to the College of Chemistry. He has enjoyed the tenure of visiting professorships at the Universities of Paris-Orsay (1979), Bordeaux (1985), Lyon (1987), Rennes (1991), Paris VI (1992), and Marseille (2000).

He has received the Adolf Windaus Medal of the German Chemical Society and the University of Göttingen (1983), the Humboldt Senior Scientist Award (1985 and 1992), the ACS Award in Organometallic Chemistry (1987), the Otto Bayer Prize (1990), the ACS Arthur C. Cope Scholar Award (1991), a Japan Society for the Promotion of Science Award (1995), the Stiftung Buchkunst Prize (1996), and the ACS Edward Leete Award (1999). He has been associate editor of *Synthesis* and is currently chief editor of *Synlett*. In 1987 he was elected to the Organic Division Committee of IUPAC.

Vollhardt has published more than 270 scientific papers or books, among the latter a sophomore textbook on organic chemistry (Freeman, 1987, 1994, 1999) that has been translated into German, French, Italian, Spanish, Korean, Japanese, and Serbian.

Scientific Sketch

The research interests of K. Peter C. Vollhardt are focused on the application of transition metals to organic synthesis. The areas under investigation range from the assembly of novel oligometallic arrays to the use of cobalt, palladium, and nickel in the construction of complex organic molecules.

A reaction pioneered by the Vollhardt group is the cobalt-mediated [2+2+2]cycloaddition of alkynes to other unsaturated substrates. Alkene, alkyne, nitrile, carbonyl, and isocyanate moieties have all served as substrates for the synthesis of a wide variety of natural products systems, including terpenes, steroids, and complex heterocycles (Fig. 1, *J. Am. Chem. Soc.* **2001**, *123*, 9324; *J. Org. Chem.* **1982**, *47*, 3447; *J. Am. Chem. Soc.* **1980**, *102*, 5253).

way, a number of potentially catalytic and conducting oligocyclopentadienyl metals (e.g., Fig **2**) with remarkable properties have become available for further exploration.

Another part of his work is concerned with the synthesis of molecules of theoretical importance, in particular, highly strained hydrocarbons and molecules with electronically destabilizing features. These include the phenylenes, a class of novel benzenoids in which benzene and cyclopentadiene are fused in an alternating manner. The cobalt-mediated [2+2+2]cyclotrimerization of alkynes provides extremely efficient syntheses of various phenylene topologies, such as linear, bent, zig-zag, angular, and triangular [N]phenylenes (Fig. **3**, *Chem. Eur. J.* **1999**, *5*, 3399; *Angew. Chem., Int. Ed.* **1999**, *6*, 800).

![Estrone and Strychnine structures]

Estrone   Strychnine

Figure 1. Natural product synthesis.

He has developed ways to attach cyclopentadienyl metal units repeatedly to other π– ligands, such as cyclopentadienyl itself. In this

![Novel transition metal arrays structures]

Figure 2. Novel transition metal arrays.

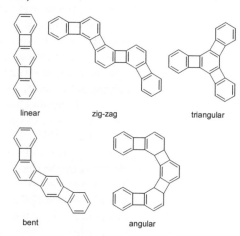

linear   zig-zag   triangular

bent   angular

Figure 3. Cobalt-mediated [2+2+2]cyclotrimerization.

Dulce de Leche

Starting materials:

1 can sweetened condensed milk

Remove the label from the can of condensed milk. Do not under any circumstances open the can yet. Take the can and stick it in a pot. Cover it with water. Put the pot on a stove and turn up the heat. Let the pot and can simmer gently for about two hours for runny dulce de leche or about four hours for solid dulce de leche.

When it´s done, open up the can and eat directly (for the solid variety) or use as a dessert spread (for the liquid variety).

NOTE:
You need to keep a close eye on the can. If it shows any signs of expansion, immediately remove it from the heat and let it cool. If you are concerned at all about the high-pressure nature of the recipe, you may poke a small hole in the top of the can and lower the water level so that the can is not completely covered. This will allow the internal pressure of the can to be released.

Reference:
http://www.milk.com/recipes/dessert/dulce-de-leche.html

«This is a recipe that reminds me of
my days in Buenos Aires.»

K. Peter C. Vollhardt

Herbert Waldmann

was born in Neuwied/Rhine on June 11, 1957. During the years
1976–1985 he studied chemistry at the University of Mainz, where
he received his Ph.D. in organic chemistry under the guidance of H.
Kunz. After a postdoctoral stay with G. M. Whitesides at Harvard
University in 1985 and 1986, he started his habilitation at the University of Mainz and obtained his tenure in 1991. In the same year he
was appointed associate professor of organic chemistry at the University of Bonn. Two years later he accepted a chair at the
University of Karlsruhe, from where he moved to Dortmund in 1999
to become both Director at the Max Planck Institute of Molecular
Physiology and full professor at the University of Dortmund.
Among several awards of high reputation, Herbert Waldmann has
received the Carl Duisberg Award of the Gesellschaft Deutscher
Chemiker (1992) and the Otto Bayer Award for outstanding research of the Bayer AG (2001). His research is documented in some
200 publications. He is editor of several books, is European Editor of
Bioorganic & Medicinal Chemistry, and is a member of the editorial
board of *ChemBioChem, Bioorganic & Medicinal Chemistry Letters, Journal of the Chemical Society, Perkin Transactions 1, Chemical Reviews*, and
the *European Journal of Organic Chemistry*.

Scientific Sketch

The scientific interests of Professor Waldmann are very broad. Apart from "classical" total synthesis of biologically potent natural products such as cyclamenol A (*Angew. Chem. Int. Ed.* **2000**, *39*, 1125), nakijiquinone C (*Angew. Chem. Int. Ed.* **1999**, *38*, 3710), and pepticinnamin E (Fig. 1, *Angew. Chem. Int. Ed.* **1998**, *37*, 1239), a major part of his work is focused on the combination of organic synthesis and cell biology.

coworkers have developed preferably enzymatic solutions in this context.

Another useful application of biocatalysts has been shown by the development of a special enzyme-labile linker that allows the release of products obtained via combinatorial synthesis from solid phase (Fig. 2, *Angew. Chem. Int. Ed.* **2000**, *39*, 1629). Furthermore, topics of asymmetric synthesis, carbohydrate chemistry, and alkaloid chemistry are investigated.

Figure 1. Pepticinnamin E.

Thus, his group has synthesized lipidated peptides and proteins (*Nature* **2000**, *403*, 223) that play an important role in the regulation of cell signaling and intracellular vesicular trafficking. Generally, synthetic approaches of such complex molecules require sophisticated protecting group techniques that offer both stability towards various reaction conditions and selective deprotection under very mild conditions (i.e., pH 6–8, room temperature). Waldmann and his

Figure 2. Waldmann's enzyme-labile safety-catch-linker for application in combinatorial synthesis.

Cinghiale in dolce e forte

Starting materials (serves 4):

1 kg wild boar haunch (without bones)

1 onion

1 clove garlic

1 carrot

2 stalks celery

1 bunch flat-leaved parsley

1 small twig rosemary

3 tbsp oil

1 tbsp flour

salt, pepper (freshly ground)

2 bay leaves

nutmeg (freshly rubbed)

100 mL red wine

125 mL consommé

1 tsp cocoa

1 tsp sugar

1 tbsp candied lemon peel

1 tbsp raisins (soaked in 10 mL Grappa)

2 tbsp pine kernels

3 tbsp balsamic vinegar

Cut meat into not-too-small cubes. Peel onion and garlic and cut them into cubes. Clean carrot and celery and cut them into cubes as well. Chop parsley and rosemary.

Heat oil in a roasting pan, add the meat, dust with flour, and roast strongly. Add prepared vegetables and herbs and steam shortly. Season with salt and pepper, add bay leaves, a pinch of nutmeg, and the red wine. Braise covered for 30 minutes at low temperature. Add hot consommé and braise for a further 30 minutes. Take out the meat and keep warm. Mash the meat roasting juices before adding the meat again.

Roast cocoa, sugar, candied lemon peel, raisins, and pine kernels in a small saucepan, quench with vinegar, and stir into the meat. Heat gently prior to serving.

Italian Cuisine – A Personal Confession

«My own cooking expertise has been confined during the years to the laboratory, particularly since my wife and I came quickly to the agreement that I
trust in her really outstanding cookery and she assigned me the privilege (and
the duty) of tasting and judging - a responsible but gladly accepted task, as
you may understand.

I want to contribute one of my favorite recipes: Wild Boar - Tuscan Way. Having the choice between French or Italian cuisine, I prefer - like the former
German Chancellor Helmut Kohl - the freshness of the Italian cuisine, which
convinces by its natural taste unadulterated by added sauces.

The attached recipe could be the main course of a delicious meal, which
should be best enjoyed at Renata´s and Mauro´s terrace in their Azienda
Agricola "Il Trebbio" in the Pratomagno hills east of Florence, while the sun
sets first behind an orange and later violet sky - at least after the
consumption of approximately 1 liter of homemade wine...

The prelude of this meal is Finocchia, a regional sausage, which should be
strongly spiced with pepper. In addition, pick some sweet ripe figs from the
surrounding trees. The combination of the pepper-salt flavor of the Finocchia
with the aromatic sweetness of fresh (!) figs is almost breathtaking. Dry regional red wine, olives, and the simple, salt-free bread from the baker on the
corner round off the starter.

Pasta is the second course. Tagliatelle in combination with pesto, the sauce
prepared from fresh herbs, parmesan and olive oil, are enjoyed by flushing
the palate with a dry Chianti. But be careful: although the Tuscany herbs are
very tasty, Mauro, being a Genovese, insists that pesto only tastes good with
basil from Genoa - the rest being inedible (I do not agree!).

Now comes the main course - wild boar. It is served cut into cubes. The combination of the game flavor with the sweet ingredients (pine kernels soaked in
Grappa, raisin, candied lemon peel, and cocoa), the balsamic vinegar, and not
to forget the garlic, produce a sensual enjoyment, a real celebration for every
gourmet. The flavor is mind-blowing, and the taste penetrates to the last
nerve – delicious. It may be accompanied by polenta, I myself prefer simply
bread, in order to avoid disharmonies. I recommend generous portioning,
since guests, based on our experience, eat more than planned. Different
wines are suitable to accompany wild boar. I recommend a Vino Nobile di
Montepulciano, which harmonizes perfectly with the light, sweet taste of the
wild boar with its mild and velvet flavor. An improvement is achieved even
with Tignanello.

After recovering from this attack to the senses, one of the few possibilities to keep the level is a dry sweet cake, for example, marble cake, accompanied with ice-cold Limoncello, a fresh, sweet, and bitter lime liqueur.

Right to the end, the cheese fans get the upper hand, and I am craving an aromatic regional product. Peccorino - dolce or forte - is my first choice. This tasteful milk product finds its not less intense equivalent in a Brunello di Montalcino, which is "a real wine for men" as a Swiss friend says.

Finally, the stressed stomach has to be supported. "Grappa" is the magic word, which - well distilled - delights the palate. I recommend Grappa di Moscato.

After such an exquisite meal, where Renata and Mauro join us as the latest to enjoy the cake with Limoncello, the conversation consists of a colorful mixture of English, Italian, German, and French, the mild night under a southern star-bright sky can become long...»

Herbert Waldmann

Ekkehard Winterfeldt

was born on May 13, 1932 in Danzig and grew up in Schleswig after the Second World War. In 1952 he began his studies in chemistry at the University of Hamburg, changing in the same year to the Technical University of Brunswick, where he received his Ph.D. in organic synthesis in 1958 in the research group of F. Bohlmann, with a thesis about the synthesis of hydroxy sparteins. Together with Bohlmann, he went to the Technical University of Berlin, where he made his habilitation in the years 1959–1962. In 1967 he was appointed associate professor, and three years later he moved to the Technical University of Hanover to become full professor and director of the Institute of Organic Chemistry. In October 2000 he became professor emeritus. In 1990 he was visiting professor at the University of California at Irvine. He has been a member of the Brunswick Scientific Society since 1983, of the Göttingen Academy of Sciences since 1984, and of the German Academy of Scientists Leopoldina, Halle, since 1996. During his scientific career, Professor Winterfeldt has received numerous awards. Among those is the Emil Fischer Medal of the Gesellschaft Deutscher Chemiker (GDCh, 1990), the Adolf Windaus Medal of the University of Göttingen (1993), the Richard Kuhn Medal of the GDCh (1995), and the Hans Herloff Inhoffen Medal (1998). In 1991 he was awarded a Doctor *honoris causa* by the University of Liège (Belgium). He was elected President of the GDCh for the years 1996–1997 and a member of the senate of the Deutsche Forschungsgemeinschaft (DFG) for the period 1995-2002. He is editor of a number of scientific journals, among those the *Journal of the Chemical Society, Perkin Transactions 1*, *Chemical Communications*, *Tetrahedron*, and *Tetrahedron Letters*.

Scientific Sketch

Ekkehard Winterfeldt´s recent research focused on enantioselective cycloadditions and their application in the synthesis of biologically active marine natural products. His aim was to mimic nature´s route to pure enantiomers. With his *Diels-Alder/retro-Diels-Alder* sequence, he developed a very useful tool to build up pure enantiomers in an efficient manner (*Chem. Rev.* **1993**, *93*, 827; *Angew. Chem.* **1995**, *107*, 489; *J. Chem. Soc., Chem. Commun.* **1996**, 887). Using this strategy the enantiomerically pure steroid **I** and its simpler hydrindan analogue **2** were prepared (Fig. I).

Figure I. Steroidal structures built up by a *Diels-Alder/retro-Diels-Alder* sequence.

The face-, endo-, and regioselective cycloadditions of the enantiopure cyclopentadienes provide a selective approach to synthesize building blocks of several marine natural products such as epi-agelorin A (*Tetrahedron* **1998**, *54*, 7273) and cephalostatin analogues (*Eur. J. Org. Chem.* **1998**, 2811; *Helv. Chim. Acta* **2000**, *83*, 1854). The cephalostatins and ritterazines, e.g., cephalostatin I (**3**) (Fig. **2**), are marine natural products isolated from the worm *Cephalodiscus gilchristi* and from the tunicate *Ritterella tokioka*. The availability from their natural sources is still limited. The outstanding cytostatic activity together with the new and interesting structure justify their total synthesis as well as the revelation of structure-activity relationships.

Figure 2. Structure of cephalostatin I.

In vitro cancer-cell-line screening provides evidence for an increased tumor-inhibiting activity of Winterfeldt's 17-*O*-functionalized analogues. Furthermore, Winterfeldt achieved the total synthesis of myltaylenol (**5**), a sesquiterpenoid alcohol bearing four chiral carbon atoms, starting from the easily available *Hajos-Wiechert* ketone (**4**), using an intramolecular *Diels-Alder* reaction (Fig. **3**, *Chem. Eur. J.* **1998**, 1480).

Figure 3. Total synthesis of myltaylenol.

One-pot Fish Soup

Starting materials:

fresh self-caught fish

assortment of vegetables

salt

pepper

parsley

dill

cream

Being a northern German coastal inhabitant, I contribute this procedure of how to prepare a fish soup. Procedure - not a recipe, because I prefer freehand cooking, without exact quantities or times - just following my feelings.

Although this fish soup is not one of my favorite dishes, it is linked to a nice little story. In his young years, our son Thomas was an enthusiastic fisher, but his prey was seldom noble or of sublime growth. Since we liked to give him the feeling of having contributed vitally to the family's nutrition and welfare, we proceeded as follows:

The fish - independent of the species - was cut and then hung by means of a fine sieve into water, in which different sorts of vegetables had been cut. The hole was cooked for a while. Then the sieve was taken out and the rest of the fish was offered to the cats without Thomas' knowledge. Salt and pepper were added, as well as parsley and lots of dill. After boiling shortly, the soup was enriched with large amounts of cream. Even the smallest fish provided a decent meal when applying this procedure.

Ekkehard Winterfeldt

Peter Wipf

was born in Aarau, Switzerland. He received his chemistry diploma in 1984 and his Ph.D. in 1987 from the University of Zurich, Switzerland, under the guidance of H. Heimgartner. His postdoctoral work as a Swiss NSF Postdoctoral Fellow with R.E. Ireland led him to the University of Virginia in Charlottesville. In 1990 he joined the faculty at the University of Pittsburgh as an assistant professor, where he was promoted to the rank of associate professor in 1995 and full professor in 1997. Among the recent awards of Peter Wipf are the Arthur C. Cope Scholar Award (1998), the Novartis Research Award (2000), and the Japan Society for the Promotion of Science Fellow Award. He is a member of the Advisory Board of *Molecules* and the *Journal of Organic Chemistry*, a member-at-large of the Organic Division Executive Committee of the American Chemical Society, and a member of the Editorial Advisory Board of *Chirality*.

Scientific Sketch

Peter Wipf's scientific interests focus on different subjects of organic chemistry, including the total synthesis of natural products, for example, the synthesis of trunkamide A (Fig. 1, *J. Org. Chem.* **2000**, *65*, 1037) and (±)–nisamycin (*J. Org. Chem.* **1999**, *64*, 5033).

Figure 1. Trunkamide A.

Dealing with organometallic chemistry, his group has a long tradition in the synthetic application of transition metals. In recent publications, he described the use of zirconocene catalysts for the asymmetric methylalumination of a-olefins (Fig. **2**, *Org. Lett.* **2000**, *2*, 1713), zirconium-zinc transmetalation, and *in situ* cata-

Figure 2. Zirconocene-catalyzed enantioselective methylalumination.

lytic asymmetric addition to aldehydes (*J. Org. Chem.* **1998**, *63*, 6454).

In the field of heterocyclic chemistry, Wipf and coworkers concentrate on the development of new stereoselective methods for the preparation of highly functionalized heterocycles, especially novel protocols for five-membered heterocycle synthesis, e.g., the use of diethylaminosulfurtrifluoride (DAST) for the cyclodehydrative conversion of β-hydroxy amides to oxazolines (Fig. **3**, *Org. Lett.* **2000**, *2*, 1165).

Figure 3. Mild cyclization of β-hydroxy amides to oxazolines.

Combinatorial chemistry and solid phase synthesis are used for reagent and catalyst design in organic and heterocyclic chemistry as well as for structure-activity analysis of bioactive compounds. Special attention is drawn to collaborative drug development for cancer therapy as previously described (*Pharm. Exp. Ther.* **2000**, *292*, 530).

In cooperation with the group of Beratan, Wipf works in the field of computational prediction of macroscopic properties, such as the assignment of the relative and absolute stereochemistry of organic molecules and the prediction of chiroptical phemomena.

³Lemon-Kiwi Pie

Starting materials (serves 4):

170 mL boiling water

1 package JELL-O brand lemon-flavored gelatine

2 tsp grated lemon peel

2 tbsp lemon juice

125 mL cold water

4 ice cubes

225 g Cool Whip, thawed

1 ready-to-use Graham cracker crust (approx. 25 cm)

½ package vanilla-flavored JELL-O instant pudding & pie filling (75 g)

170 mL milk

1–2 kiwi fruit

shamrock candy sprinkles

Pour 170 mL of milk into large bowl. Beat ½ package. JELL-O instant pudding & pie powder and 225 g thawed Cool Whip whipped with wire wisk for 1 minute. The pudding should become very viscous. Spread it with a spoon across the bottom of the Graham cracker crust. Refrigerate for 20 minutes.

In the meantime, stir boiling water into gelatin in large bowl at least 2 minutes or until completely dissolved. Stir in lemon gratings and juice. Mix cold water and ice and add to gelatin, stirring until slightly thickened. Remove any remaining ice. Stir in the remaining whipped topping with wire wisk until smooth. Refrigerated for 20–30 minutes or until mixture is very thick and will mound. Spoon into Graham crust on top of vanilla pudding layer. Cut 1–2 kiwis into slices and spread over the top. Decorate with shamrock candy sprinkles.

Refrigerate for 6 hours or overnight until firm.

Peter Wipf

Yoshinori Yamamoto

was born in Kobe/Japan on November 21, 1942. During the years
1962–1970 he studied chemistry at Osaka University, where he received his Ph.D. in organic chemistry under the guidance of I. Mori-
tani. He was appointed instructor at Osaka University in 1970.
While working as an instructor, he went to H. C. Brown's group at
Purdue University as a postdoctoral associate (1970–1972). In 1977
he was appointed associate professor at Kyoto University. In 1986
he moved to Tohoku University, Sendai, to become professor of
organic chemistry. He also holds a professorship at IMRAM (Institute
of Multidisciplinary Research for Advanced Materials), Tohoku
University, and a visiting professorship at Kyushu University. He is a
recipient of the Chemical Society of Japan Award for Young Chemists (1976) and the Chemical Society of Japan Award (1995) and also
received the Dortmunder-Gambrinus Award from the University of
Dortmund (1999) and the Humbold Research Award (2002). For his
research on boron neutron capture therapy, he received the Hiroshi
Hatanaka Lectureship from the International Society of Neutron
Capture Therapy (1996). He is the regional editor of *Tetrahedron
Letters* and he was the President of the International Society of
Heterocyclic Chemistry (2000–2001).

Scientific Sketch

The scientific interests of Yoshinori Yamamoto are divided into three categories.

The first covers the development of new synthetic methods with *Lewis* acid and transition metal catalysts.

Shortly after the opening of the "*Lewis* acid age," he introduced a new concept in organocopper chemistry in 1977 (*J. Am. Chem. Soc.* **1978**, *100*, 3240); a *Lewis* acid such as BF₃·OEt₂ dramatically increases the reaction rate and changes the selectivities of a conjugate addition reaction of an organocopper reagent (*Angew. Chem. Int. Ed.* **1986**, *25*, 947).

Beginning about 10 years ago, his contribution to the research field of transition metal-catalyzed, especially palladium-catalyzed, organic synthesis became prominent. He developed the palladium-catalyzed addition of pronucleophiles to C-C multiple bonds of unsaturated compounds such as allenes, alkynes, enynes, and methylenecyclopropanes (*Chem. Soc. Rev.* **1999**, *28*, 199). By applying the above mentioned *Lewis* acid-allylstannane methodology, hemibrevetoxin B was synthesized (Fig. 1).

Figure 1. Hemibrevetoxin B.

Furthermore, the ring skeleton of gambierol has been constructed by the *Lewis* acid-promoted one-shot synthesis of two ring segments (Fig. **2**, *J. Am. Chem. Soc.* **2001**, *123*, 6702).

Figure 2. Gambierol.

The third field of research is an organochemical approach to Boron Neutron Capture Therapy (BNCT) in cancer treatment. He has a keen interest in this interdisciplinary research between organic chemistry and biochemistry and has developed several very important boron carriers (Fig. **3**).

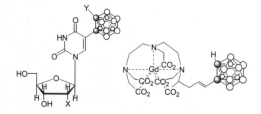

Figure 3. Drugs in BNCT: glycoside and Gd-157.

Some of the compounds were tested in vivo and exhibited better therapeutic results compared to the compounds utilized clinically until now.

Tofu Tempura

Starting materials (serves 6):

350 g tofu

flour or cornstarch

oil

125 mL of dashi stock or chicken broth

60 mL light-colored soy souce

15 mL mirin (Japanese sweet rice wine for cooking)

1 tsp cornstarch

water

Simple to make, nutritious, and tasty

The tofu, made from soybean and very popular in Japan (perhaps also available in Europe and the US), is drained. Usually, it is sold in a pack containing water. The tofu is placed on a cutting board and tilted to one side, or placed between two sheets of paper towels, in order to remove the water from the surface of the tofu.

The tofu (13 x 10 x 7 cm; about 350 g) is cut into fourths and coated with cornstarch or all-purpose flour.

Deep-frying oil is heated around 175 °C. The temperature control of the oil is important. Tofu, covered by flour (or cornstarch), is put into the heated oil and fried until the surface color changes to lightly brown. Tofu tempura is picked up and drained with paper towels.

The tempura sauce is prepared. Although usually it is commercially available, the preparative procedure is as follows:

(i)   dashi stock or chicken broth,

(ii) light-colored soy sauce,

(iii) mirin, which is a Japanese sweet rice wine for cooking,

(iv) 1 tsp cornstarch plus 1 tsp water.

The four starting materials (substrates) are mixed in the order of (i)-(iv), and a very nice sauce is prepared. Tempura sauce ingredients are put into a small sauce pan and heated until sauce thickens. Tofu tempura is placed in an individual bowl and the sauce is poured over.

Scallion, ginger root, and/or bonito flakes are sprinkled, if you like. Even without these additives, tofu tempura is tasty.

Of course, together with this tofu tempura, drinking beer (or wine) is very enjoyable, and hopefully fruitful to arouse one's vitality for doing research and administrative work, ... on the next day.

«I am living alone in Sendai. Fortunately or unfortunately, my wife lives in Kobe and the distance between Sendai and Kobe is about 1000 km! Additionally, my three kids live separately: one in Brussels and the other two in Tokyo. So, all the family members of Yamamotos are living separately. Usually, I take a supper with my students at the university cafeteria, but on Saturday and Sunday I have to manage a dinner/supper by myself. The easiest way to do this task is to go to a restaurant, of course, or to go to shops in the basement floors of department stores since there are so many different types of dishes. However, sometimes, I cook by myself at home; the most important criterion in this case is whether or not the procedure is simple and the product is nutritious and tasty.»

Yoshinori Yamamoto

Axel Zeeck

was born in Rummelsburg (Pomerania, today in Poland) in 1939 and studied chemistry at the Georg August University Göttingen. He obtained his Ph.D. in 1966 under the guidance of H. Brockmann. In 1974 he finished his habilitation also in Göttingen, where he became assistant professor of organic chemistry in 1980. In 1999 he was appointed full professor of Biomolecular Chemistry.

He is coordinator of the Lower Saxony research focus "Marine Biotechnology" and is responsible for the chemical education of medical students. In this context, he is author of the book *Chemie für Mediziner* (Chemistry for Medical Students) (Urban & Fischer, 4th ed., 2000). In 1994 he was awarded the Max Planck Research Award of the Max Planck and the Alexander von Humboldt Society – one of the most reputable German scientific awards – for his exploration of the mechanism of the effect of bafilomycin and concanamycin on the V-type ATPase. He is the author of some 150 publications; 35 patents have been issued to him.

Scientific Sketch

Microorganisms are an important source of novel natural products such as antibiotics and other active substances. For the isolation of chemically new and biologically active compounds, the group of Zeeck cultivates especially actinomycetes, streptomycetes, and fungi imperfecti. In the search for new secondary metabolites, both the biological and the chemical screening have been applied with success. For the latter either thin-layer chromatography (TLC) with different types of staining reagents or HPLC with varying detection methods (UV, MS, CD) is used to record all metabolites produced in the culture extracts. Most of the strains evaluated in Zeeck's group are isolated from earth samples and are cultivated in fermenters of up to 50 liters.

As a result of such efforts, hexacyclinic acid, a natural product of highly complex structure, has been isolated and characterized recently (Fig. 1, *Angew. Chem. Int. Ed.* **2000**, *39*, 3258).

H₃C, OH
O
H H H H
H H
CH₃
O OH
HO
O O H
O
CH₃
H H CH₃
COOH

Figure 1. Hexacyclinic acid, from *S. cellulosae.*

The chemical work starts with the isolation and structure elucidation of the novel natural products. Structural problems are solved by using modern spectroscopic methods (e.g., MS, high field 2D-NMR, X-ray analysis). Zeeck and co-workers have revealed the structures of several hundreds of metabolites that belong to different chemical classes (e.g., peptides, macrolides, quinones, glycosides, and polyenes).

Further investigations focus on the biosynthesis of the discovered compounds, starting with feeding experiments using stable isotope precursors. Thus, the biosynthesis of kendomycin, a polyketide isolated from *Streptomyces violaceoruber* with a unique structure, was disclosed. This molecule shows antiosteoporotic properties and is an inhibitor of endothelin receptors. By using feeding experiments with marked precursors, the biosynthesis was elucidated (Fig. **2**, *J. Chem. Soc. Perkin Trans. I* **2000**, 323 and 2665).

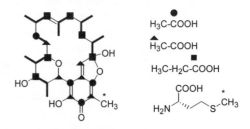

H₃C-COOH
H₃C-COOH
H₃C-H₂C-COOH
COOH
H₂N S CH₃

Figure 2. Kendomycin, from *S. violaceoruber.*

The group is interested in new biosynthetic pathways and tries to modify the metabolites by applying the precursor-directed biosynthesis and by changing the cultivation conditions (OSMAC approach, *ChemBioChem* **2002**, *3*, 619). The biological activity of the metabolites and derivatives is established in different test systems, mostly in cooperation with colleagues and industry.

Filled Peppers à la Benjamin

Starting materials (serves 2):

bell peppers (yellow or red, 1–2 per person)

crumbled brown bread

crème fraîche

curry powder

herbs

1–2 eggs

double cream

cheese slices

salt

1) Wash the peppers and hollow them out from the stem so that a hole for the filling is formed.
2) Fill half of the pepper with the crumbled wholewheat bread.
3) Prepare the rest of the filling in a separate bowl: crème fraîche, salt, curry, herbs, eggs, some double cream.
4) Pour filling into the pepper and add some more crumbled bread if necessary.
5) Cover the opening with a slice of cheese.
6) Put the filled peppers into a pot and add so much vegetable broth that the lower half of them is plunged. Boil 15–20 minutes with closed lid until the peppers are soft.

To be served with rice or millet.

«Being short on time due to changing the diapers, nursing, comforting, and carrying, this recipe originates from the plight, after the birth of our son Benjamin (14.10.2001), to bring something palatable and vegetarian onto the table.
Meanwhile, we are both capable of preparing this dish, but the result is always slightly different, which might result from a different handling of the spices...»

Sabine Fischer & Axel Zeeck

Index

Index